God's Covenants

God's Covenants

•

*Expositions of Bible Doctrines Taking
the Epistle to the Romans as a Point of Departure*

Volume 8

Romans 9:1–11:36

Donald Grey Barnhouse

William B. Eerdmans Publishing Company
Grand Rapids, Michigan

Wm. B. Eerdmans Publishing Co.
4035 Park East Court SE, Grand Rapids, Michigan 49546
www.eerdmans.com

© 1963 The Evangelical Foundation, Inc., Philadelphia, Pennsylvania
All rights reserved under International and Pan-American and Universal Copyright Conventions

Originally published 1963
This edition published 2023

ISBN 978-0-8028-8368-1

Library of Congress Cataloging-in-Publication Data

A catalog record for this book is available from the Library of Congress.
LCCN 58013516

Quotations from J. B. Phillips, *The New Testament in Modern English*, copyright 1958, are used by permission of The Macmillan Co., New York.

Quotations from the Revised Standard Version of the Bible, copyright 1946, 1952, by the Division of Christian Education of the National Council of Churches, are used by permission of Thomas Nelson & Sons, New York.

Τῷ ἀγαπῶντι ἡμᾶς καὶ λύσαντι ἡμᾶς
ἐκ τῶν ἁμαρτιῶν ἡμῶν ἐν τῷ αἵματι αὐτοῦ

Rev. 1:5

Contents

	Preface	ix
I	Paul's Desire for Israel	1
II	Israel's Position	7
III	The Messiah, God and Man	17
IV	Children of the Promise	23
V	Children of Mercy	32
VI	The Children of Sovereignty	41
VII	Righteousness—the False and the True	53
VIII	The Righteousness of Faith	59
IX	Salvation for All	70
X	The Word for the World	77
XI	God's Disobedient People	86
XII	The People of the Promise	95
XIII	When God Hardens Hearts	103
XIV	Israel's Future Glory	110
XV	Broken Branches	119

CONTENTS

XVI	The Times of the Gentiles	127
XVII	Israel's Deliverance	135
XVIII	The Mercy of God	142
XIX	The Mind of God	148

Preface

Again it gives me great joy to present to the faithful readers of Dr. Barnhouse, *God's Covenants*, the eighth volume of his series of studies of the whole Bible, taking as his point of departure the Epistle to the Romans.

In chapters nine through eleven, Paul's main purpose, as seen in the light of the whole epistle, is to demonstrate that his great teaching on justification, sanctification and the assurance of the believer, set forth in the first eight chapters, is not to overlook the blessing or restoration which is to come to his ancient people, Israel. These chapters show that God has not cast off His people, but that His ultimate purpose includes the fulfillment of every promise made to them.

Dr. Barnhouse has grasped these great truths and presented them in his own inimitable way.

I wish to thank Miss Olive DeGolia and Miss Mildred Horner for assisting me in the preparation of the manuscript.

If you are blessed by reading this book, will you remember the continuing ministries of the Evangelical Foundation in your prayers?

—Ralph L. Keiper
Director of Research, Evangelical Foundation

I

Paul's Desire for Israel

I say the truth in Christ, I lie not, my conscience also bearing me witness in the Holy Ghost, That I have great heaviness and continual sorrow in my heart. For I could wish that myself were accursed from Christ for my brethren, my kinsmen according to the flesh (Rom. 9:1–3).

As we turn to the opening verses of the ninth chapter, one of the most poignant cries that ever rose from a human heart is now set before us as the apostle bares his heart and shows that he was truly willing to be separated from God, accursed by Christ, if only others whom he loved could be saved and go to heaven. What has happened here? Why is there such a break in thought? What is the explanation for this sudden change from joy to sorrow? In the concluding verses of the eighth chapter, we read: "Who shall separate us from the love of Christ? Shall tribulation, or distress, or persecution, or famine, or nakedness, or peril, or sword? Nay, in all these things we are more than conquerors through him who loved us. For I am persuaded that neither death, nor life, nor angels, nor principalities, nor powers, nor things present, nor things to come, nor height, nor depth, nor any other creation shall be able to separate us from the love of God, which is in Christ Jesus our Lord." What joy! "I say the truth in Christ, I lie not, my conscience also bearing me witness in the Holy Spirit, that I have a great heaviness and continual sorrow in my heart. For I could wish that myself were accursed from Christ for my brethren, my kinsmen according to the flesh." What sorrow! Thus we ask, Is there a sudden break in the thought of the Apostle Paul? No, there is a smooth continuity here, and all the more revealing when we come to realize its true essence.

A question has arisen, not only in the mind of the apostle, but in the minds of all who have read the Old Testament and have been introduced to the truth of the New Testament. "You say that there is no separation from the love of God? Then, what about us, the age old people of God. Have we been supplanted by the coming of Christ in favor of a Gentile people?"

Aaron's Altar Replaced

In the light of this, it is understandable that Paul should cry out with sorrow because of the state of his brethren. He knew that God had replaced the lambs of Aaron's altar with the Lamb of God, Jesus Christ. He knew that Christ had died so that the blessing of Abraham might come upon the Gentiles (Gal. 3:14). He had seen the transformation in many Gentiles when the Holy Spirit brought the love of God to them in an overwhelming stream. He knew that there was light for all the dark multitudes of earth because God had given the Lord Jesus to be the Light of the world (John 8:12). He himself had been raised in the strictest sect of the Pharisees, and had believed in the Old Testament so firmly and so simply that he murdered anyone who transgressed its precepts. He was present when Stephen was stoned to death. The charge against Stephen was brought by false witnesses who said, "This man constantly speaks blasphemous words against this holy place [the temple in Jerusalem], and wants to change the customs which Moses delivered us" (Acts 6:14). Stephen had replied with a great summary of the history of Israel, showing that the fathers of his accusers had killed the prophets who announced "the coming of the Just One," the Lord Jesus Christ (Acts 7:52). Paul had heard these truths and had seen Stephen die. It was not many days before he himself, while in pursuit of further victims, was stopped by God on the road to Damascus. From then on, he was in the hands of God as the apostle to the Gentiles, and he brought us the only hope that any Gentile can ever have.

Love for Israel

But, though God had called Paul to be a minister to the Gentiles, there are many evidences in the New Testament, and none more important than those to be found in the chapters before us, that Paul had a continual desire to work with his people. This is quite understandable. Paul was a Jew, and very proud of his Jewishness, proud almost to the point of sin. We can well understand that, since he has before him a subject that deals with the theological status of his own people, his whole heart and mind gush forth under the inspiration of the Holy Spirit to explore the many questions that revolve around the many purposes of God for Israel and for the Gentiles. One of his themes will be to reconcile the fact that the Old Testament is filled with specific promises to the Jews with the fact that the New Testament is filled with the doctrine of the melting of the Jews and Gentiles together into the new body, the Church. The first thing that Paul does on approaching so grand a theme mixed with so many controversial subjects is to tell the Israelites that he loves them well enough to be willing to be cursed by Christ if only they could be brought to the knowledge of the salvation which he now possesses. We must not forget that the people of Israel had a remarkable training in their Scriptures, and almost immediately they would be forced to think of the other man in their history who asked God to destroy him, but to save people. There are two men in the Bible, Moses and Paul, who honestly were prepared to ask God to send them to hell if only others could be saved. Here is a love that can come from but one source. Such a love does not arise in the heart of man by nature. It comes only from Jesus Christ.

This was the heart of God pouring itself out in the utter fullness of love. And it was a Rock from which flowed the stream that caused Moses and Paul to turn their hearts inside out before men, and to show that they would have been willing to be separated from divine love and come under the divine curse if only the wandering ones of earth would come back to the Father.

THE GOLDEN CALF

It was this same love that caused Moses to be willing to be lost if only the wrath of God could be kept from falling on His people. The story is told in the book of the Exodus. God had brought the children of Israel to the foot of Mount Sinai where He planned to give them the tables of the law and the plan of the tabernacle with its means of approach to Him. A thick cloud came down upon the mountain and Moses was called of God to move up the mountain into the cloud. The New Testament tells us that the mountain burned with fire, and was in blackness, darkness, and tempest. The people could not endure that which was commanded. If so much as a beast touched the mountain it was to be stoned, or thrust through with a dart. So terrible was the sight that even Moses said, "I exceedingly fear and quake" (Heb. 12:18–21).

As the days went by and Moses did not return, the people grew restless and impatient. They remembered the worship which they had known in Egypt, the worship of Apis, the bull, and they called upon Aaron to make an idol for them. He had them give him all of their gold, and there was enough to make a calf.

Upon the mountain the Lord was speaking with Moses. He knew, of course, what was going on down at the foot of the mountain and spoke to Moses in wrath.

CHAPTER I

There is a play of words here that would be humorous if the scene were not so tragic. "The Lord said to Moses, Go, get you down; for the people, whom you have brought out of the land of Egypt, have corrupted themselves" (Exod. 32:7).

The Lord went on speaking of the guilt of the people until Moses interrupted with a cry of prayer, "Lord, why does your wrath wax hot against your people whom you have brought forth out of the land of Egypt with great power and with a mighty hand?" (v. 11).

"They are your people," God says to Moses. "They are your people," Moses says to God. Neither God nor Moses wanted them in the condition in which they were at that moment, naked and dancing around an image of a calf in the midst of the camp.

Moses' Plea

In wrath Moses broke the tables of the law which God had given to him. Moses knew that the sin of the people deserved the utmost of the wrath of God, but now we see him in one of the most sublime acts ever performed by man. On the next day Moses started back up the mountain with a great determination in his heart. He reached the top and began to speak to the Lord. The original Hebrew is most poignant. It is a sigh, a groan, and a cry. It is a sentence that has no ending. Even in our King James Version the translators left the end of the sentence trailing, with a dash for its punctuation. It was a sentence that was strangled in the middle with the sobs of the man who was asking to be sent to hell if only the people might be spared the righteous judgment of God. We read, "And Moses returned unto the Lord, and said, Oh, this people have sinned a great sin, and have made them gods of gold. Yet now, if thou wilt forgive their sin—" At this point the sentence stops and the translators end it with a dash.

There must have been a long silence at this point. Moses was recognizing the perfect righteousness of God. He was realizing to the full that the wages of sin is death. He was understanding that sin had to be punished and he did not want this people to be punished. God had called the people his and Moses had replied that they were the Lord's people. Now he realized fully that they were also his people and he loved them. Suddenly there came to his mind the thought that God could not pardon such sin as he had seen in the camp, with naked men dancing around a golden calf and singing that this was the god that had brought them up out of the land of Egypt. Then his cry begins again, "And if not, blot me, I pray thee, out of thy book which thou hast written" (Exod. 32:31, 32).

It must not be forgotten that God had already told Moses, the day before, that if he would step aside God would destroy the people utterly and make a new people from Moses. This could have been a great temptation to a lesser man; one of the subtlest of all temptations is for a man to wish to perpetuate himself in his sons as though there were some special clay in his mixture. This is a sin that must be repented of if ever our children are to become something before God. His gifts are because of grace and not because of race.

Moses did not yield to the temptation for a moment. He had been as a woman in travail, laboring to bring forth this people. He had gone through the agony of the various meetings with Pharaoh and had seen the weakness of the people. Hidden in the Greek verb in Hebrews eleven, there is a great insight into the heart of Moses. We read, "Through faith he kept the passover" (Heb. 11:28), but it would be better translated, "Through faith he instituted [began] the passover. . . ." It was as though he realized that with this tenth plague the children of Israel would be forced out of Egypt and that he would suddenly become as a lonely nurse with more than a million rebellious charges. But he did not draw back. Now that the people had brought themselves into a position where the just wrath of God should strike them, he puts himself between them and the divine wrath and cries, "Blot me, I pray thee, out of thy book which thou hast written."

Jerusalem Doomed

Every Jew knew this story. Then, across the centuries, Israel stood again at a place where they deserved the wrath of God. They had killed the prophets and stoned those who were sent unto them. By raising monuments to the prophets who had been killed, they confessed that they were the children of those who had killed the prophets (Matt. 23:29–30). Before Jesus died, He cried out, "O Jerusalem, Jerusalem, thou that killest the prophets, and stonest them that are sent unto thee, how often would I have gathered thy children together, even as a hen gathereth her chickens under her wings, and ye would not" (Matt. 23:37).

Years passed. Paul must have known the inner reality of Christ's prophecies against the city of Jerusalem. Paul must have known that Christ had said, "And when you see Jerusalem compassed with armies, then know that its desolation is nigh . . . for there shall be great distress in the land, and wrath upon this people. And they shall fall by the edge of the sword, and be led away captive into all nations; and Jerusalem shall be trodden down of the Gentiles until the times of the Gentiles be fulfilled" (Luke 21:20, 23, 24).

CHAPTER I

The point of my story is that Paul knew all this and sensed that the terror was about to descend upon the people. The ominous rumblings of the hatred between Rome and Israel could already be heard. It is at this moment that Paul cries out in agony, "For I could wish that myself were accursed from Christ, for my brethren, my kinsmen according to the flesh."

"Blot me out of thy book," Moses cried to God on Sinai as he saw the arm of judgment raised. "Curse me, O Christ, for my brethren, my kinsmen according to the flesh," cries Paul.

A Cry of Love

The thing that Moses prayed for and that Paul prayed for could not be theirs. Neither Moses nor Paul could be the Savior of men because they were nothing more than men. Moses was a sinner—a murderer, in fact. Never forget that God put the Ten Commandments into this world by the means of the hands of a murderer. Paul was a sinner, and he, too, had taken human life. Neither of them could be forgotten by God and cursed. Only one could undertake that work and become a curse.

Both Moses and Paul understood the exceeding evilness of sin. Both understood that nothing could atone for sin except the removal of the sin by placing it on a substitute and there striking it with the ultimate curse. Both understood this, and both prayed God to strike them if only His wrath might be turned away from those whom they loved.

We must go to the book of Galatians before we can find the truth fully expressed. We read there, "As many as are of the works of the law are under the curse; for it is written, Cursed is everyone that continueth not in all things which are written in the book of the law to do them" (Gal. 3:10). And, when man is seen in that desperate state, one appears who is the Lamb without spot and blameless. No sinful man but the sinless Son of God alone is eligible to die for others. Therefore, we read the triumphant cry, "Christ has redeemed us from the curse of the law, being made a curse for us; for it is written, Cursed is everyone that hangs upon a tree, so that the blessing of Abraham might come upon the Gentiles through Jesus Christ" (Gal. 3:13, 14).

II

Israel's Position

Who are Israelites; to whom pertaineth the adoption, and the glory, and the covenants, and the giving of the law, and the service of God, and the promises; whose are the fathers, . . . (Rom. 9:4, 5)

In considering our text, it is important that we define our terms. These brethren over whom Paul yearned, these kinsmen according to the flesh, are called Israelites. It was to Israel who had come from the loins of Abraham that God gave the adoption.

To the Israelites belongs the adoption. God had all of the families of the earth before Him. In His inscrutable wisdom and grace, He chose Abraham. "Hearken to me, you who follow after righteousness, you who seek the Lord; look to the rock from which you were hewn, and to the quarry from which you were digged. Look to Abraham your father, and to Sarah who bare you; for I called him when he was alone, and saved him, and increased him" (Isa. 51:1, 2).

"Now the Lord had said unto Abram, Get thee out of thy country, and from thy kindred, and from thy father's house, unto a land that I will shew thee. And I will make of thee a great nation, and I will bless thee, and make thy name great; and thou shat be a blessing. And I will bless them that bless thee, and curse him that curseth thee: and in thee shall all families of the earth be blessed" (Gen. 12:1–3). If we examine this set of promises, we shall see that some are unconditional and some are conditional. "I will bless thee" is an unconditional promise; "Thou shalt be a blessing," or as the Hebrew says, "be thou a blessing," is also unconditional. The other two promises are conditional: "I will bless them that bless thee," and "I will curse him that curseth thee."

CHAPTER II

The privileges of Israel set forth in our text are so intertwined that it is impossible to sort them out. The adoption, the covenants, and the promises are all so involved with each other, that I shall treat them together.

God's Dealings with Abraham

The entire Bible, both the Old and the New Testaments, is filled with references and allusions to the choice of Israel for definite purposes in the plan of God. We find that from the beginning God acted toward Abraham and his seed in a special manner. He took him, for example, into His secret when He was about to destroy Sodom. God had said to Himself, "Shall I hide from Abraham that thing which I do, seeing that Abraham shall surely become a great and mighty nation, and all the nations of the earth shall be blessed in him?" (Gen. 18:17, 18). Nehemiah prayed, saying, "Thou art the Lord, the God who chose Abram . . . and gave him the name of Abraham" (Neh. 9:7). Isaiah received a revelation from God in these terms: "This people have I formed for myself; they shall show forth my praise" (Isa. 43:21). Stephen, the first martyr of the Christian Church, recounted the history of God's people in the address for which he was killed, saying, "The God of glory appeared unto our father, Abraham, when he was in Mesopotamia, before he dwelt in Charran, And he said unto him, Get out of your country, and from your kindred, and come into the land which I will show you" (Acts. 7:2, 3).

The promises to Abraham included the possession of the land of Israel, and a great deal more which Israel has never yet possessed. The original land grant is recorded in the fifteenth chapter of Genesis, and is one of the most fascinating stories in the Bible. When we consider that the present war tension in the Holy Land between Israel and the Arab world goes back to this original promise and pledge by God, we can realize its continuing importance for our day.

Abraham had made a great spiritual choice. In the previous chapter, it is recounted how he had given up the booty which might have fallen to him after the defeat of the four kings. He said that he would not take so much as a thread or a shoelace, lest anyone should say that he had made Abraham rich. He had, by faith, come to depend completely upon God. Immediately, God appeared to him and announced that He was Abraham's shield and exceeding great reward (Gen. 15:1). Abraham reminded the Lord that he was childless, and the Lord promised that his seed should be as numerous as the stars of the sky and the sands of the sea. The Lord then added a promise concerning the land: "I am the Lord that brought you out of Ur of the Chaldees to give you this land for an inheritance" (Gen. 15:7). Once more Abraham asked God a question: What evidence would he have that he would inherit the land? The answer is astonishing. When it is understood, it is nothing short of an oath that is confirmed to Abraham by God Himself with a blood sacrifice, reminding us of the death of Christ, as the symbol of the guarantee. God said, "Take a heifer three years old, and a three year old ram, and a turtle dove and a young pigeon." This is one of the strangest answers that was ever given to a question. Yet, as we shall see, it was the only possible answer. Question: How shall I know that I shall inherit the land? Answer: Take me a heifer. One might think that the dial of the radio had slipped from one program to another. The question comes from a program where people are seeking legal advice. The answer comes from a broadcast of the department of agriculture. The heifer and the inheritance are bound together in the mind of God, and this reply is the only possible answer. The heifer is to be killed and its blood is to be shed. The Lord is really saying that the guarantee of the title to the land of Israel is nothing short of the cross of Jesus Christ. The promise of the land is guaranteed by this symbol of the cross of Christ.

A Solemn Oath

In our courts men are asked to take an oath upon a Bible; in the courts of Islam, men swear by the beard of the prophet Mohammed. In ancient times the dividing of animals was a most solemn method of taking an oath, as both Greek and Roman authors state. The parties to the oath divided the animals into two halves, cutting it down the back bone, and walked around the two heaps in the path of a figure eight. God severely judged the men in the time of Jeremiah who broke their covenant after having "cut the calf in twain and passed between the parts thereof" (Jer. 34:18–20). God does not take or make oaths lightly.

The Lord began to teach Abraham that the land would be occupied against much opposition. The prophecy has been verified in many ways. Egypt sought to keep Israel away from the land; the forces of Canaan made them a prey; the forces of Greece and Rome fought against the Jews, and there are not wanting enemies today who oppose their entrance to Palestine. There are those who would take these promises to Israel and "spiritualize" them. I believe these prophecies are to be taken literally and that they will be fulfilled in God's good time.

The covenant that was given to Abraham concerning the possession of the land was preceded by a sentence which shows God's desire for faith on our part. "Know of a surety," He tells Abraham (Gen. 15:13). God never wants His children to know a thing halfway. He has made provisions for us to know things with deep certainty. "How shall I know?" Abraham asks. God points to the sacrifice and says, "Know of a surety."

CHAPTER II

The Sacrifice

The sacrificial animals lay in two heaps, ready for the taking of the oath. God did not permit Abraham to take part in the oath of the covenant. Abraham had to stand by and watch God go through the solemn motions of ratification. If men had been making a mutual covenant, both parties would have moved in the figure eight among the pieces, but God alone moves here. The covenants of God are not agreements between parties meeting and agreeing on mutual terms. The promises of God begin and end with Himself. They are unilateral agreements, divinely and blessedly one-sided. God promises, God blesses, God gives, God guarantees, God assures, and, since He is "willing more abundantly to show unto the heirs of promise the unchangeableness of his counsel" (Heb. 6:17), God confirms it by an oath.

First Abraham saw a smoking furnace move between the pieces of the sacrifice. This is the same symbol of God's presence by which He appeared to Moses on Mount Sinai when the law was given to Israel (Exod. 19:18). The furnace was well known to ancient peoples, being the small apparatus with which the silversmiths and the goldsmiths melted down their precious metals so that the dross might be separated from the refined and pure elements. The trial of our faith is much more precious than gold which perisheth though it be tried in the fire (1 Pet. 1:7). The Lord is with His own in the furnace (Dan. 3:25). The smith who thus purifies metal keeps the fire burning until the dross comes to the top. He removes this until the molten metal is clear enough to reflect his own face. God told His people in the last book of the Old Testament that He would sit as a refiner and purifier of silver (Mal. 3:3), and the furnace will burn until He sees His image in His people.

The second symbol of the confirmation of the oath was that of the burning lamp. This is again Himself, since we are told that God is light and in Him dwelleth no darkness at all (1 John 1:5). All of this, the blood sacrifice, the oath of God, the smelting furnace, and the burning lamp, was symbolic of the Messiah, the Lord Jesus Christ. When the Lord Jesus told us that Abraham rejoiced to see his day and was glad (John 8:56), we may well believe that it was at the time of this covenant. Thus the promises were guaranteed to Israel.

The Land and Its Boundaries

It was in these circumstances that God said, "I have given thee this land" (Gen. 15:18). Since all of the promises of God are sure, "given" is in the past tense. In the light of this promise and covenant, guaranteed by the symbols of the death of the Savior, Israel's title deed to the land is sure and certain. God has told us that we are to pray for the peace of Jerusalem, for He will fulfill His promise to Abraham as He restores Israel to the land for His glory.

When God gave the land to Abraham, He defined the boundaries with a scope that is amazing when we look at it in the light of the historical occupation of Palestine by Israel. The boundaries of the land include the territory from the river of Egypt to the great river, the Euphrates. It includes the land once occupied by a multitude of tribes, including the Hittites. These were the sons of Ham, and their territory centered in what is now Turkey—Asia Minor.

God's Protective Covering

Behind this text lies one of the most amazing stories of the Bible. The glory that belonged to Israel was something very special—a glory which all Jews understood, and which was such a part of their history that it must have made a profound impression on the whole nation. The glory was a visible thing. It came upon Israel from the beginning of its march as a nation, stayed through many centuries, was taken from them in judgment, but shall be theirs once again in the future.

The first mention of the glory is to be found in the description of God's protective covering over His people at the moment they came out of Egypt. We read, "And the Lord went before them by day in a pillar of cloud to lead them along the way, and by night in a pillar of fire to give them light, that they might travel by day and by night; the pillar of cloud by day and the pillar of fire by night did not depart from before the people" (Exod. 13:21, 22). This was not a cloud in the same sense that a meteorologist defines a cloud. We can understand that they called it a cloud, just as in our generation there has appeared a new thing which our world has called a cloud, but which is not a cloud. When men split an atom and start the chain reaction of a nuclear explosion, there rises a vast thing—a thing which has been called a "mushroom cloud." It has the shape of a mushroom and the form of a cloud. It would have been better called a "toadstool cloud," for it is a thing of death. Certainly, it is no more cloud than it is mushroom, and the showers it sends down are showers of death. We can quite understand that our journalists have called it "a mushroom cloud," and we can, in like manner, understand that the people in the day of the exodus, called the thing that God sent before them "a cloud." Later on in their history they called it by another name, the *shekinah*, which means the "glory." Though that word is not found in the Hebrew of the Old Testament, coming, as it does, from the Talmudic literature, it has, nevertheless, been adopted into the common language of theology and is well-known among Bible students. This cloud, this *shekinah*, this "glory," is the matter that is spoken of here in Romans as one of the precious possessions of Israel.

In the Wilderness

When the army of Pharaoh pursued the children of Israel, the latter thought that they were going to die, for they were hemmed in with the desert to the north and to the south, the Red Sea to the east, and Pharaoh's army to the west. The children of Israel despaired because they looked north, south, east, and west. Only Moses looked up and there was Jehovah God, ready to show Himself strong on behalf of His chosen people. Moses said to the people, "Stand still, and see the salvation of the Lord which he will show to you this day" (Exod. 14:13). "Then the angel of God who went before the host of Israel moved and went behind them; and the pillar of cloud moved from before them and stood behind them, coming between the host of Egypt and the host of Israel. And it was a cloud and darkness to them, but it gave light by night to these; so that the one came not near the other all night" (vv. 19, 20).

When the army of Pharaoh had been destroyed in the Red Sea after the children of Israel had passed safely through, the cloud began to lead the people of God and continued before them throughout the forty years of their wandering. There is every evidence that this cloud spread out over the people like a covering canopy in order to protect them and to provide shelter for them. What happened during these forty years is one of the most remarkable series of events, if not the most remarkable, in all of God's dealings with His people throughout the centuries. Yet, if you asked the average Sunday school teacher, or even the average minister, to name the half dozen great miracles in the Bible, it is probable that ninety per cent of them would fail to mention the miracle of the cloud and all that went on beneath it. Beyond question, it was a greater miracle than those performed by Moses against Egypt and greater than the series of miracles performed by Elijah or Elisha.

The climate of the desert of Sinai is one of the most changeable on earth. Travelers who have spent time there know that it is necessary to have a fully equipped expedition in order to penetrate its fastnesses. Its mean temperature by day, throughout the entire year, will run to one hundred and fifty degrees Fahrenheit, so that it would be impossible to sustain human life there for any length of time. During the night the temperature falls to below freezing, so that there is a change in temperature of about a hundred and fifteen degrees in any twenty-four hour period. There is neither water nor food there. It would be impossible to keep any considerable number of people alive there without having a complete chain of supplies.

Israel's Position

As the children of Israel moved into the desert where they were to receive the law, where they were to reject God at Kadesh Barnea, and where they were to wander for thirty-eight long years, the cloud was spread over them, supernaturally. David tells us in the Psalms, "He spread a cloud for a covering; and fire to give light in the night" (Ps. 105:39). The true picture is an astounding one. We know from the book of Numbers that there were 603, 550 men of arms, over twenty years of age. The total population cannot have been less than two and a half or three millions of people. The cloud, the "glory," had to be spread out over a considerable space to cover this vast group of people as they traveled in the desert. The city of Philadelphia has approximately the same population as the number of people that traveled for forty years without food and water except that which was provided by God. The stem of the cloud came down upon the tabernacle, and the cloud billowed out over the countryside to form the protection for the people.

We read how the cloud was designed to lead them. "On the day that the tabernacle was set up, the cloud covered the tabernacle, the tent of the testimony; and at evening it was over the tabernacle like the appearance of fire until morning. So it was continually; the cloud covered it by day, and the appearance of fire by night. And whenever the cloud was taken up from over the tent, after that the people of Israel set out; and in the place where the cloud settled down, there the people of Israel encamped; as long as the cloud rested over the tabernacle they remained in camp. Even when the cloud continued over the tabernacle many days, the people of Israel kept the charge of the Lord and did not set out. Sometimes the cloud was a few days over the tabernacle . . . and sometimes the cloud remained [only] from evening until morning . . . or it continued for a day and a night; when the cloud was taken up they set out. Whether it was two days, or a month, or a longer time, that the cloud continued over the tabernacle, abiding there, the people of Israel remained in camp and did not set out; but when it was taken up, they set out" (Num. 9:15ff.).

Over the Mercy Seat

When we study the cloud of glory more closely, we find that it was associated with the sacrifice of the blood which was shed for the remission of sins. Whenever the priest brought the sacrifices into the holy of holies, once a year on the day of atonement, it was seen that the stem of the cloud of glory was down on the cover of the ark where the blood was applied. This place was called the mercy seat, the place of propitiation, or the place of atonement. The revelation of this fact was given to Moses after Aaron's two sons had been struck dead for approaching this place of glory with fire that had not been lighted at the altar of sacrifice. We read, "Tell Aaron, your brother, not to come at all times into the holy place within the veil, before the mercy seat which is upon the ark, lest he die; for I will appear in the cloud upon the mercy seat" (Lev. 16:2).

When the people murmured against God and the wrath of God was kindled against the people, God, in His training of Moses, brought him face to face with the possibility of severe judgment upon the people. The Lord even suggested that the people should be destroyed and that God would make another people from Moses. But Moses answered the Lord and reminded Him that the Egyptians would hear of it and laugh at God, for, said Moses, "They have heard that thou, O Lord, art seen face to face, and that thy cloud stands over them and that thou goest before them, in a pillar of cloud by day and in a pillar of fire by night" (Num. 14:14). Thus Moses pleaded that the Egyptians would believe that God was not able to finish what He had started and this became the basis of Moses' appeal for the Lord's continuing grace. Surely the glory belonged to Israel.

We do not know the full history of the cloud of glory. It would appear that, after the children of Israel entered into the promised land, the cloud of glory was restricted to its presence inside the tabernacle. When Solomon dedicated the temple, the glory was once more present and filled the house. "Now when the priests came out of the holy place . . . and when the song was raised, with trumpets and cymbals and other musical instruments, in praise to the Lord, for he is good, for his steadfast love endures forever; the house, the house of the Lord, was filled with a cloud, so that the priests could not stand to minister because of the cloud; for the glory of the Lord filled the house of God" (2 Chron. 5:11, 13).

The Glory Removed

There came a time, however, in the days of Ezekiel, when the iniquity of the people was overflowing, that the Lord took the symbol of glory and removed it to Heaven. Even though it went, the memory of it still lingered and when Paul, hundreds of years later said, "to Israel belongs the glory," they remembered this glory of which they had been told in their childhood. In the prophecy of Ezekiel, there are several references to the appearance of the glory in the sight of Ezekiel. Then there comes the sad day when the glory-cloud is removed. We read, "And the glory of the Lord went up from the cherubim (*i.e.*, the ones of which those on the mercy-seat were the symbol) to the threshold of the house; and the house was filled with the cloud, and the court was full of the brightness of the glory of the Lord" (Ezek. 10:4). After thus moving from the holy place to the court and the threshold, we find that, in a little while,

Israel's Position

"The glory of the Lord went forth from the threshold of the house, and stood over the cherubim (which the Lord had let Ezekiel see) and the cherubim lifted up their wings and mounted up from the earth in my sight as they went forth . . . and the glory of the God of Israel was over them" (v. 19). Then, after another interval, the cloud was removed to the top of the Mount of Olives, from whence it departed to Heaven. We read, "Then the cherubim lifted up their wings . . . and the glory of the Lord went up from the midst of the city, and stood upon the mountain which is on the east side of the city . . . Then the vision which I had seen went up from me" (Ezek. 11:22–24).

AT THE BIRTH OF CHRIST

The glory was not seen again until the moment the infant Jesus was born in Bethlehem. The shepherds that were watching in the fields by night were the next to see it. "For the glory of the Lord shone round about them, and they were filled with fear. And the angel said to them, 'Fear not; for behold I bring you good tidings of great joy which shall be to all people. For unto you is born this day in the city of David, a Saviour, which is Christ [Messiah] the Lord'" (Luke 2:9–11). Even as Ezekiel had seen the glory go from the house of the Temple to the Mount of Olives, and from thence into Heaven, so the Lord Jesus went to the Mount of Olives and, we read, "He ascended into heaven, and the cloud received him out of their sight" (Acts 1:9).

There is no visible cloud. By faith we know that glory in Christ, "For it is the God who said, 'Let light shine out of darkness,' who has shone in our hearts to give the light of the knowledge of the glory of God in the face of Christ" (2 Cor. 4:6).

AT THE SECOND COMING

But when the Savior Messiah comes again, once more the cloud of glory shall appear. At the second coming of Christ, believers will be "caught up together in the clouds to meet the Lord in the air" (1 Thess. 4:17). We must never think of this as hiding in rain clouds, but as entering into all the glory of God, forever. Finally, the triumph of Christ at His second coming will bring a full manifestation of the cloud of glory. We read Christ's own statement: "Then will appear the sign of the Son of man in heaven, and then all the tribes of the earth will mourn, and they will see the Son of man coming on the clouds of heaven with power and great glory" (Matt. 24:30). In another place He speaks of His return as "coming in the glory of my Father" (Mark 8:38).

CHAPTER II

The Bible comes to an end with the book of the Revelation of Jesus Christ, and it is announced, "Behold, he is coming with the clouds, and every eye will see Him, everyone who pierced him; and all tribes of the earth will wail because of him" (Rev. 1:7). Then the Lord will restore Israel and bring peace on earth in His way and through His chosen people. Once more the cloud of glory will appear on the earth. We read in the prophecy of Isaiah, "Then the Lord will create over the whole site of Mount Zion, and over her assemblies, a cloud by day, and smoke and the shining of a flaming fire by night; for over all the glory there (*i.e.*, in that place) will be a canopy and a pavilion. It will be for a shade by day from the heat, and for a refuge and a shelter from the storm and rain" (Isa. 4:5, 6).

III

The Messiah, God and Man

And of whom, as concerning the flesh, Christ came, who is over all, God blessed forever, Amen (Rom. 9:5).

Of all the privileges and advantages that were ever given to God's chosen people, the greatest by far was that they should be the people from whom God would bring the Savior, the Messiah, the Redeemer, the Deliverer, the Lord Jesus Christ. We have examined the other glories that belonged to Israel—the adoption as a nation, the glory of constant guidance with the presence of God, the covenants of promise that came to them through Abraham, the giving of the law through Moses, the service of the Temple through Aaron, and all the multitudinous promises which could never be compassed in a series such as this. Now the apostle rises to the greatest of heights and shows the supreme blessing that belonged to Israel. They were the children of those who are called "the fathers," namely, Abraham, Isaac, and Jacob, who were more highly favored than any member of the human race. They were the objects of God's direct grace, and had their names added to the attributes of deity. We may know God as our Creator and Lord. We may know Him as Redeemer and Savior. We may speak to Him and call Him, "My God," but no one else will think of Him as particularly the God of any individual. It would be impossible for me to say, "The God of Donald Barnhouse." It is not only possible, it is divinely decreed that God may be called the God of Abraham, the God of Isaac, and the God of Jacob. He Himself announced that He was not ashamed to be called the God of Abraham, Isaac, and Jacob (Heb. 11:16).

Far above all such honors and benefits which may be considered as *personal*, there is added another blessing which must be considered as infinitely exceeding all others, a blessing in which the entire world is interested. This is nothing less than that "of whom, as concerning the flesh, Christ, Messiah, came, who is over all, God blessed forever." Charles Simeon wrote of this, "Yes, when the ever-blessed, the co-equal, the co-eternal Son of God came into the world, that by His own obedience unto death, He might accomplish the redemption of sinful man; He assumed His human nature from them, even from a Jewish virgin. In a more strict and appropriate sense than any other person, a Jew may say of Jesus, He is bone of *my* bone, and flesh of *my* flesh.

"Consider now how glorious these distinctions were. To what other nation was any one of them ever vouchsafed? Or what has the greatest monarch upon earth that can be in any degree compared with them? The honors which come of man are lighter than vanity itself when compared with those which come of God. When weighed in this scale, the highest monarchs in the universe are not so elevated above a slave as the lowliest Jew is exalted above them. But what shall we say to the giving birth of the Messiah, who was 'the Mighty God,' 'Emmanuel, God with us?' Here all words fail us. In vain does the imagination attempt to grasp so wonderful an event. 'God manifest in the flesh!' How 'great this mystery of godliness!' and how infinitely ennobled are that people, to whom the everblessed God is so nearly related!"

God and Man in One Person

When we come to the present text in Romans, we cannot say much for the more modern translation, though the marginal reading is again extraordinary. The King James Version reads, as we have seen, "Of whom, as concerning the flesh, Christ came, who is over all, God blessed forever." The main text of the revision inserts a false punctuation mark to make it read, "of their race, according to the flesh, is the Christ." The period does not belong there. The revision continues, "God, who is over all, be blessed for ever." This could be interpreted as a separation between the two persons of the Father and of the Son, and certainly it is a weaker translation. The revisors have followed Goodspeed, Moffatt, and even the American Standard Version, who render it in the same fashion. In his note on the passage in the Companion Bible, Bullinger remarks, "To account for various readings, the RV (and he means the English Revision of 1881), sometimes appeals in the margin to ancient authorities, meaning Greek manuscripts, but here, and here only, *modern interpreters* are allowed to introduce, by varying punctuation, devices for destroying this emphatic testimony to the deity of the Lord."

All of the important ancient translations, including the Vulgate, Luther's German version, Calvin's translation, and the rest, follow that which is in the King

James Version. It must be added that the Revised Standard Version has a footnote that is even stronger than the King James Version, for they translate it, "of their race, according to the flesh, is the Christ, who is God over all, blessed for ever." Moule states that no other translation than the traditional one would ever have been suggested if it had not been for historical controversy. Surely the Greek cannot be fairly translated in any other way than an ascription of deity to the Lord Jesus Christ. The great Delitzsch translates it into German, *Christus, nach dem Fleisch, welcher ist Gott uber alles, hochgelobt in Ewigkeit*—"Christ, according to the flesh, who is God over all, highly blessed for ever." He goes on to say that the whole of the verse teaches that Christ was God and man in the same person.

It is easy to understand why the deity of the Lord Jesus Christ is set forth at this particular point in the narrative. Paul is expressing amazement that his people had not seen the light which so blinded him on the road to Damascus. His people had not seen the great wonder of the incarnation of God in Christ. It was this blind rejection of the Lord Jesus Christ that both degraded his people from their natural supremacy and prepared the way for the manifestation of the wisdom and power of God in calling the Gentiles into the Church. The very foundation of the Church is that Name of Jesus Christ as God which is both rejected and glorified. The people whom God chose for His own have rejected the Name, but God has given Christ the Name that is above every name. Before that Name every knee shall bow and every tongue shall confess that Jesus Christ is the Lord Jehovah (Phil. 2:10, 11).

There are several passages in the Bible where the humanity and the deity of the Lord Jesus Christ are clearly placed together. We have examined this at some length in our earlier studies in Romans. In the first chapter we have it recorded that the gospel was about the Lord Jesus Christ, God's Son, "who was made of the seed of David according to the flesh; and declared to be the Son of God with power, according to the Spirit of holiness, by the resurrection from the dead" (Rom. 1:3, 4). There is something to be added at this point in our study of the epistle.

The Author of the Bible was never afraid to put contradictory ideas and doctrines into the same verse. This is, perhaps, one of the divine ways of telling us that we cannot judge truth after the logic of Aristotle. This should not astonish men of science in our day since men in astrophysics speak of a curved universe and tell us that the farthest stars may be very, very near to us if we can learn the shorter route! I do not know enough about it to be sure that my illustration is exact, but the paradox is not unknown in many branches of human thought. In the Bible we find verses which speak doctrinally of the humanity and deity of Christ: "For unto us a child is born, unto us a Son is given" (Isa. 9:6); we find the human child born and the divine Son given. In the New Testament we find, in addition to the earlier Romans passage, "In the fulness of time God sent forth his Son, made of a woman, made under the law" (Gal. 4:4) and there, once more, we see the deity that is sent forth and the humanity that is made.

There are also verses which do not express doctrines but which give us illustrations of the two natures of our Lord Jesus in such fashion that we cannot fail to be struck by the contrast. What is more human than paying taxes? What is more divine than having them paid by sending an apostle on a mission that combines supernatural knowledge with supernatural power to catch a fish that has a coin in its mouth sufficient to pay the tax? (Matt. 17:24–27). What is more human than for a Man to be so fatigued with work that He falls asleep in a boat on the sea of Galilee—so fast asleep that He is not awakened by a storm that frightens even seasoned fishermen? What is more divine than to have the Man, awakened from His sleep by the frightened fishermen, speak with authority to the attacking waves and bring a great calm to the sea in a way that causes men to lose their fright and to have it replaced by a holy awe that makes them worship the Lord, saying, "What manner of man is this, that even the winds and the waves obey him?" (Matt. 8:27)? Again and again we see this throughout the four Gospels: the human Jesus wanders away from His parents and the divine Lord confounds the teachers in the Temple (Luke. 2:41–50); the human Jesus administers a mild rebuke to His mother for interfering in things which do not concern her and then turns, a little later, to change the water into wine (John 2:1–11); the human Jesus leaves the disciples that He may go and pray and the divine Jesus walks to them on the water (Matt. 14:22–33); the human Jesus dies—surely there is nothing more human than death—and He dies in a divine way, head held high to the last moment even though the blood had been drained from His body, crying with a loud voice even though He had been in anguish for the six hours of the crucifixion.

God the Son

Our text in Romans clearly leads us to contemplate this remarkable person who was both descended from the Jewish fathers according to the flesh and God over all, blessed forever. Some interpreters who sought to diminish the translation of this text did so on the grounds that Paul in his writings always holds Jesus as subordinate to the Father, never giving Him a title higher than "the Son of God," and that, therefore, he would not give Him a higher title in this verse. How can anyone who has studied all of Paul's thought believe for an instant that Paul had any idea of Christ less than that of His being eternally God the Son? Only in this sense can we realize the absolute uniqueness of the Lord Jesus Christ. He was not mere man who had discovered a high relationship with God; He was the Lord of Glory, the eternal Lord God of Hosts who had come in the likeness of sin's flesh, being made man according to the family of these whom He honored, calling them His "fathers." He was the eternal Word made flesh dwelling among us. John was inspired by the Holy Spirit to write similar truths. "In the beginning was the Word, and the Word was with God, and the Word was God" (John 1:1). Nothing could be stronger and nothing less will suffice.

Paul certainly equaled this thought in his first letter to Timothy. There we read, "And without controversy great is the mystery of godliness: God was manifest in the flesh, justified in the Spirit . . ." (1 Tim. 3:16). Here again, the revisors have not followed true scholarship in their translation but have allowed an interpretation to creep into the text at the expense of the Greek, and have relegated scholarship to a footnote. They translate, "Great indeed, we confess, is the mystery of our religion: He was manifested in the flesh." The footnote reads, "Greek: *who*, other ancient authorities read *God*; others *which*." They must know that only the manuscripts which smell of Arianism, the ancient name for unitarianism, give pronouns, while the best authorities, without question, read, "God was manifest in the flesh."

We can understand Paul's classifying this among the mysteries which he describes in several of his writings. When the Bible speaks of a "mystery," it is not using the term in our modern sense which applies the word to a story of crime being unraveled or of some other unknown matter being brought to light. A mystery in the time of the New Testament was a truth which had been hidden in the past and had suddenly become revealed in its most intimate details. Surely this applies to the incarnation of God in Jesus Christ. The Old Testament had many prophecies of the Lord Jesus but they are clearer to us because we are looking at them after their fulfillment and because we have the clear light of the New Testament to reveal to us their inner meanings. Abraham, Moses, David, Isaiah wrote of the coming of the Messiah, but they did not see Him as we know Him, living as we do on this side of the cross and the open tomb. To take one example, Isaiah wrote of a sign that should come to Israel through the conception of a child by an *almah* (Isa. 7:14). It is very improbable that Isaiah or anyone else ever applied this to the Messiah until the time of Christ. Mary knew the origin of her child in reality; she knew that Jesus did not have a human father, but Mary probably did not know the theological meaning of what was happening, for she "pondered these things in her heart" (Luke 2:19), and "marveled at those things that were spoken of him" (Luke 2:33).

The Mystery Understood

It was only as the Holy Spirit began to teach the early Christians these truths at the mouths of the apostles that the mystery was understood. Our responsibility is all the greater because we live after centuries of study of the Word of God, centuries which have brought so much more light to illuminate the truth.

Finally, there is one more passage which must be considered. When Paul was nearing the end of his ministry, he passed through Ephesus and the elders of the church followed him out of town to speed him on his way. The story of their farewell and his parting admonitions is a great and tender one. In the midst of it is a counsel which declares the person and work of Christ in its highest degree. "Take heed therefore unto yourselves, and to all the flock over that which the Holy Spirit has made you overseers, to feed the church of God, which he has purchased with his own blood" (Acts 20:28). Once more it must be noted with sadness that the revisors have passed by the highest textual authorities and gone to the lesser manuscripts, tainted with Arianism, calling it the church of the Lord instead of the church of God. Paul was calling Jesus Christ by the high name of God, even as God Himself had done in the Psalms, quoting it again in the epistle to the Hebrews, "Unto the Son he says, thy throne, O God, is for ever and ever" (Ps. 45:6, 7; Heb. 1:8). Someone may ask, could Paul speak of the church of God which He purchased with His own blood? Can we speak of the blood of God? No question could bring out in a higher degree the true nature of the being of the Lord Jesus Christ. In Him was combined the perfection of what humanity should have been with all that was the eternal Lord Jehovah of Hosts. Thus in Christ dwelt all the fullness of the Godhead bodily (Col. 2:9).

This is the glory above all glories that accrues to the Lord's people, Israel. It was Jewish flesh that was accepted by God the Savior. It was thus that Jesus shed the divine blood upon this earth. Before we are through with these studies, the Lord willing, we shall see that the Lord Jesus has not cast off this people and that He intends to come again and restore them to the place that has been promised to them through all of history. Of Israel, as concerning the flesh, came Christ. God over all, blessed forever.

IV

CHILDREN OF THE PROMISE

Not as though the word of God hath taken none effect. For they are not all Israel, which are of Israel: Neither, because they are the seed of Abraham, are they all children: but, in Isaac shall thy seed be called. That is, they which are the children of the flesh, these are not the children of God: but the children of the promise are counted for the seed. For this is the word of promise, at this time will I come, and Sarah shall have a son. And not only this; but when Rebecca also had conceived by one, even by our father Isaac: (For the children being not yet born, neither having done any good or evil, that the purpose of God according to election might stand, not of works, but of him that calleth;) It was said unto her, the elder shall serve the younger. As it is written, Jacob have I loved, but Esau have I hated. (Rom. 9:6–13)

Our text begins by showing that the rejection of Christ as God and Messiah is not a contradiction of the Scriptures. We read, "Not as though the word of God hath taken none effect." The revision says, "It is not as though the word of God had failed, for not all who are descended from Israel belong to Israel." The people of that time desired to lower the Messiah to the level of their own desires. How terrible it was to take advantage of His grace in order to despise His Person and His glory! It was natural that the Israel of Paul's day should have resented the Gospel as it was preached to the Gentiles by Paul. Such preaching would seem to nullify the pledges of God which He had made to their fathers. How could there be any security for them if the Messiah had already come, if He had been rejected by them, and if He had bid His true followers turn to the Gentiles? Was there not conflict between the Gospel promises to the Gentiles and the ancient promises to the earthly people?

If there was going to be such human reasoning, Paul would take them back to the very beginning of the promises and show them that salvation did not come

CHAPTER IV

merely through being a physical descendant of Abraham. At the very origin of the story of the chosen people, there is the account of God's election of one brother and his rejection of the other. If Israel was going to presume that being a child of Abraham was all that mattered, they were brought face to face with the fact that Abraham had another child, Ishmael, and that he was cast out and refused a place in the promises of God. If the contemporaries of Paul were going to admit that only the children of Isaac should have the inheritance, they were face to face with still another elective choice. One of the sons of Isaac was rejected and another was put in his place. Esau, the elder son, was not to inherit, but Jacob, the younger son, was to receive the promises. At once we see, therefore, that the selection is tied to the promises of God and not to the fleshly line of Isaac.

Abraham's Children

What Christ said to Nicodemus is true throughout all generations: "That which is born of the flesh is flesh" (John 3:6). Christ had met this same objection with the Pharisees. They had confronted Him, as recorded in the Gospel of John, angered because He spoke of freeing them. They cried out that they were Abraham's seed and had never been in bondage to any man (John 8:33). This is one of the most curious verses in the Bible. I know of no other which will better show the brazen effrontery of members of the human race toward God. The Pharisees of Christ's day were claiming on the grounds of their fleshly descent from Abraham that they had never been slaves of anyone. If we go to their history, we remember that they were slaves in Egypt for four hundred years. A little further on we discover, after they have been brought into the promised land, that they are constantly in and out of slavery to the Philistines. It was necessary for God to raise up judges a score of times to redeem them from the slavery of this alien people who were pre-empting the land they had come to possess. As time went on, they were captive to Babylon for seventy years. The armies of the Hittites, the Egyptians, the Babylonians, and other nations overran them again and again. Alexander the Great conquered them and one of his generals took possession of the land after his death. Soon the Roman legions were victorious over the remnants of the Greeks and the Romans were ruling Palestine even when Christ was born. For these leaders of a people with so long a history of recurring slavery to stand up in the face of Christ and protest that they had never been in bondage to any man would be ludicrous even if it were not so tragic.

There may be multitudes of Abraham's descendants but they are not all the children of Abraham. There is a vast difference between flesh and spirit. This is not merely a question of human genealogy; this is a question of eternal salvation. The argument, therefore, is one that shuts the mouth of the objectors. Since they do not want to include the children of Ishmael and the children of Esau, they cannot accept the doctrine of the necessity of God's promise and God's elective call.

Furthermore, there was a difference between the two children who were excluded from the elective promises by God. Abraham had begotten both Ishmael and Isaac. God had refused one of the sons and had acknowledged the other. There might have been those who predicted this choice on the worthiness or unworthiness of the mother. One of the mothers had been an Egyptian slave girl and the other had been Sarah, wife and princess of the whole line of promise. They might take pride in such an ancestry and reject Ishmael with contempt. When God makes His next selective, elective choice, He does it between two sons who are still in the womb of the same mother—twin sons! There are no human values here. It cannot be said that one of the boys was superior to the other. The pronouncement by God was made before the children were born. Neither of them had done any good or evil. The authority for the election lay in the heart of God. There is no possible human way to account for it.

Sovereign Grace

The text flatly states that the choice of God was not dependent on their birth or their character. The choice was in the heart of God and based entirely on His sovereign authority. He decided that Jacob was the child who was to carry the line of Messiah and be the heir to blessing, and in the same way, He determined that Esau was not to carry the line nor inherit the blessing. How foolish are those who try to limit God to time and make Him dependent upon the actions of men! The election of those who have been chosen by God is not governed by the foreseen superiority of a Jacob to an Esau. This simply is not true. Jacob had done no good that could recommend him to God and Esau had done no evil that could have disqualified him. Before these twins came from their mother's womb, the sovereign God of the universe who decides all things had determined that the elder should serve the younger. This was God's divine purpose. The works and characters of the individuals had nothing to do with the choice. In fact, they are explicitly excluded so that all of the reason for the call shall rest in God Himself, who is the One who calls.

This passage has been the center of much controversy, but its implications are so definite that it is difficult to see why men reject the truth—except that they are so filled with prejudices that they do not wish to accept anything that will controvert that which they wish to believe. It is true that the doctrine taught here has been pushed by some beyond what is written. Calvin was very guilty at this point.

CHAPTER IV

He attempted to deduce from this passage what has come to be called "double predestination." The Bible nowhere announces the predestination of the lost. It would seem that Calvin and others have drawn an inference in purely human logic. They would hold that the choice of Jacob implies the reprobation of Esau. Both of these brothers were born in sin; they both had the nature of Adam. They both grew up in sin. They both were children of wrath, disobedient by nature. If there had been any merit in these two sons, God would have been unjust in not rewarding that merit. The choice of one deserving man over another deserving man would have been favoritism. When we see that the two were equally undeserving, the whole picture becomes different. Everything that is said in the entire Bible about the nature of fallen man may be said—must be said—about both Jacob and Esau. God determined, for causes that are to be found in Himself and have not been revealed to us, to show favor to Jacob. This is grace and grace alone. To show grace to one does not imply condemnation of the other. The condemnation had been equally upon both since the fall of Adam. The grace that is now manifested is sovereign.

Those who have criticized this passage have not realized that the question about the two sons does not come from the book of Genesis where the story was originally told. There is not a line in Genesis to the effect that the Lord hated Esau. All that we read there is the following: Rebecca was barren and Isaac prayed for her. Soon she was with child and the twins in her womb struggled together. She prayed about it and the Lord said to her, "Two nations are in your womb, and two peoples, born of you, shall be divided; the one shall be stronger than the other, the elder shall serve the younger" (Gen. 25:23). This is sovereign grace in action. God determined a course of action and announced it because it pleased Him to announce it. The choice of Jacob did not predestine Esau to be lost. There was no announcement of hatred against Esau at this moment in his history. A thousand years passed before the Lord God announced that He hated Esau. By that time it had been made manifest to all the world that in the heart of Esau's descendants there was nothing but unrelenting hatred against the Lord's chosen people. Esau, himself, had wept about his personal rejection of the birthright and its privileges. He had sought repentance carefully with tears, but there was not found place for repentance (Heb. 12:17). It may be that some day I shall find a verse in the Bible that will make me decide, finally, that Esau was personally a lost soul. I have not yet found such a verse. I do know that he was rejected as far as the birthright was concerned, but the hating was pronounced upon his descendants. The verse that is quoted here in Romans is from the last book in the Old Testament. When Malachi begins his prophecy we read, "I have loved you," says the Lord. But you say, "How hast thou loved us?" To this God answers, "Is not Esau Jacob's brother? Yet I have loved Jacob and I have hated Esau; I have laid waste his hill country and left his heritage to the jackals of the desert."

Children of the Promise

THE MESSIAH PROMISED

From this contrast of texts, one from the first book of the Old Testament and the other from the last book of the Old Testament, comes the paragraph which we are now considering. This wide range of prophecy concerning the promises to Jacob, his election, and the inheritance goes far beyond their lives in Palestine. In the beginning the promise was not fulfilled. Jacob had to flee; and when he returned, he did so with the sufferance of Esau. He came, tremblingly, asking for forgiveness at the hand of his brother. He was afraid for his very life; and when he was forgiven, he lived for years on the bounty of his brother. Where did Esau ever serve Jacob? Where did this elder ever serve the younger? There was something far greater than the social position of the elder son involved in this election and its consequent promises. In the days of David and Solomon, the children of Israel had a temporary victory over the sons of Esau. The prophet Balaam was forced against his will to announce the far greater victory that would be Jacob's: "A star shall come forth out of Jacob, and a scepter shall rise out of Israel; it shall crush the forehead of Moab, and break down all the sons of Sheth. Edom shall be dispossessed, Seir also, shall be dispossessed, while Israel does valiantly" (Num. 24:17, 18). Following this, there is the announcement of the Messiah Himself, "Out of Jacob shall come he that shall have dominion."

That the election and promises go even beyond the first coming of the Savior is shown by the prophecies which contrast the descendants of the two brothers in the far distant future. Even today in Palestine, Ishmael and Esau block the road of the line of Isaac. After the second coming of Christ, Jacob shall reign over Israel—and over Esau. That it is a prophecy of the future is certain, for Isaiah speaks of the change that shall come upon the animal world when the wolf shall dwell with the lamb and when poison shall have been taken from the serpents. This dates the prophecy beyond question. Then we read, "In that day the Lord will extend his hand yet a second time to recover the remnant which is left of his people . . . He will raise an ensign for the nations, and will assemble the outcasts of Israel and gather the dispersed of Judah from the four corners of the earth . . . They shall put forth their hand against Edom and Moab (these are the descendants of Esau), and the Ammonites shall obey them" (Isa. 11:6, 11, 12, 14).

ONE WAY OF SALVATION

The Lord Jesus, when bringing His message of judgment against the leaders of His day, said, "I tell you, many will come from east and west and sit down at table with

CHAPTER IV

Abraham, Isaac, and Jacob in the kingdom of heaven while the sons of the kingdom will be thrown into the outer darkness" (Matt. 8:11, 12). There is no dispute among interpreters here concerning the parties mentioned in this judgment. The many who come from the east and the west are the Gentile believers of our age. The sons are the children of Israel. Why should they be cast into outer darkness? As we have pointed out before, all Israel are not of true Israel. These doubtless were Israelites after the flesh, and not after the spirit.

We have seen that there are no racial distinctions in God's sight. Both Jews and Gentiles are by nature the children of wrath, children of disobedience, dead in trespasses and sins. In the third chapter of this epistle are many quotations from the Old Testament describing the fallen state of man. Nicodemus, the leader of Israel, may have been astonished at the teaching of Christ when he spoke of the necessity of the new birth, but he certainly was not astonished at the statement, "that which is born of the flesh is flesh, and that which is born of the spirit is spirit" (John 3:6). The Lord rebuked Nicodemus because as a master of Israel he should have known about the new birth.

From the Garden of Eden until our day and beyond until the end of God's dealings with fallen man, there has been, there is, and there shall be but one way of salvation. Abraham looked forward to the Lord Jesus Christ and was saved through Him even as we look backward to the Lord Jesus Christ and are saved through Him. Christ said, "Abraham rejoiced to see my day; and he saw it, and was glad" (John 8:56). Moses made his choice because he esteemed the reproach of Christ greater riches than the treasures of Egypt (Heb. 11:26). When the Lord asked the Pharisees whose son the Messiah was to be, they answered rightly that He was to be the Son of David. To this Jesus replied, "How is it then that David, inspired by the Spirit, calls him Lord?" (Matt. 22:43). With these verses in mind, we do not need to go further in stating that not only did Abraham, Moses, and David receive promises about the Savior, and believe promises about the Savior, but they believed in the Savior Himself. It is also evident that throughout Israel's history the true people of God brought typical sacrifices of blood by faith, though they did not understand the wonderful details by which God was to fulfill those sacrifices. It was because of the bringing of these sacrifices that they received remission of sins, not that there was anything in the animal sacrifices, but that there was everything in the sacrifice of the Son of God.

So it was from the gate of Eden, "by faith Abel offered unto God a more excellent sacrifice than Cain, by which he obtained witness that he was justified" (Heb. 11:4). This same process applies to all those who believed before the time of Christ, as we have shown in great detail. We saw that the true meaning of the death of Christ was that He should be "set forth to be a mercy seat through faith in his blood; to declare God's righteousness for the remission of sins [of Old Testament saints] through the forbearance of God" (Rom. 3:25). Thus it can be seen that a true Israelite is one who took God at His word and lived in obedience to Him.

Oneness of Believers

We must ask one further question: Shall those who were equal sharers with the Gentiles in Adam's fallen nature and who received the same condemnation that we received and who were given the promises of the Redeemer, even as we were given them, and who showed their faith in Christ by bringing the sacrifices that were commanded by God to prefigure His Son, and who were made alive by the same Holy Spirit who has made us alive—shall these believers of the Old Testament times share with us the same glory that is set before us who live in this age since Pentecost? To answer this question, we again return to the words of our Lord as He spoke words of judgment to the leaders of His day. "I tell you, many will come from east and west and sit down at table with Abraham, Isaac, and Jacob in the kingdom of heaven while the sons of the kingdom will be thrown into the outer darkness." We are to sit down with the children of Israel in glory in the fulfillment of this promise. Abraham, Isaac, and Jacob will sit at the high table. Whatever supplementary interpretations may be given to this passage, it cannot be disputed that the sons of the Old Testament are to sit down and feast in the glory of the kingdom of heaven, or as Luke puts it, "the kingdom of God" (Luke 13:29).

Whatever may be the differences between Israel living on the earth before Christ and the believers living on the earth since Christ, there can be no doubt that they are here seen united in glory. They may well have had different privileges, and we undoubtedly have the great blessing of the indwelling Holy Spirit, but we see them joined to us, "to reign in life through the one man, Jesus Christ". We see that "those whom he foreknew he also predestined to be conformed to the image of his Son, in order that he might be the firstborn among many brethren. And those whom he predestined he also called; and those whom he called he also justified; and those whom he justified he also glorified" (Rom. 8:29, 30). It is one unbreakable chain. We are one with Abraham in this justification. If we go from this backward or forward, the result is the same. We were justified together because we had been called together. The calling was because of the mutual predestination, and the mutual predestination was because we were alike joined in the foreknowledge of God. If we proceed from our common justification in the future direction, we find that we are glorified together. All who believe are justified from all things (Acts 13:39), and all who are justified are glorified. Beyond this glorification for Abraham and all his seed, there can be nothing higher. We share and share alike.

The great resurrection chapter of 1 Corinthians 15 likewise joins the Old Testament saints and the New Testament saints in a single resurrection. Paul is showing the importance of the resurrection—if Christ be not raised we are still in our sins. "Then those also who have fallen asleep in Christ have perished. If in this life only we have hope in Christ, we are of all men most to be pitied. But in fact Christ has been raised from the dead, the first fruits of those who have fallen asleep" (1 Cor. 15:18–20). Surely Abraham is among those who had fallen asleep in Christ, and he and all who were of like faith shall be raised with Christ at His coming. Could we ask anything more for ourselves? The Old Testament saints and the New Testament saints, alike having borne the image of the earthly, shall alike bear the image of the heavenly.

Jews and Gentiles

When we come to the epistles to the Galatians and to the Hebrews, there is so much material on these subjects that it would require special articles to cover both of them. A brief summary must suffice. Paul was writing to the Galatians because of the Judaizers who were teaching them that they were inferior to Abraham and that they could not have the higher glory that was promised to him unless they returned to the law of the Old Testament and received circumcision. Certainly, if it were true that there is a position and promise of glory for the church that is higher than that of Abraham and his seed, here was the place to announce it. The epistle merely sets forth that we and Abraham were justified in exactly the same manner. Christ bore the curse so that the blessing of Abraham might come upon the Gentiles (Gal. 3:14). It is added that the Gentiles who are saved in this age will get the common blessing promised to Abraham, "they who are of faith are blessed with faithful Abraham" (Gal. 3:9). Even a human contract cannot be broken if once it has been agreed upon; how much less the divine contract! The climax is that "we are all the children of God through faith in Christ Jesus" (Gal. 3:26). Then comes the astonishing revelation—astonishing when we consider the divine order—that because we belong to Jesus Christ we have become Abraham's seed (Gal. 3:26, 29).

In the eleventh chapter of Hebrews, Israel's hall of fame, we see magnificently displayed the faith of the men of the Old Testament. It is stated that "God is not ashamed to be called their God, for he has prepared for them a city" (Heb. 11:16). In the Greek it is not merely *a* city but "*the* city which hath foundations, whose builder and maker is God" (Heb. 11:10). That city can be none other than "the city of God, the new Jerusalem" (Rev. 3:12). This city, the holy Jerusalem, is the bride, the Lamb's wife, having the glory of God (Rev. 21:10, 11), and it must be noted that though the wall of the city has twelve foundations, which are the twelve apostles, the city has twelve gates, which are the twelve tribes of Israel (Rev. 21:12; 14). What glory and what joy to be joined with these beloved of God, these men of faith of all ages! They obtained a good report through faith, yet received not the promise, God having provided some better thing for us (what glory is hidden in that cryptic phrase?) "that they without us should not be made perfect" (Heb. 11:39, 40).

V

Children of Mercy

What shall we say then? Is there unrighteousness with God? God forbid. For he saith to Moses, I will have mercy on whom I will have mercy, and I will have compassion on whom I will have compassion. So then it is not of him that willeth, nor of him that runneth, but of God that showeth mercy. For the Scripture saith unto Pharaoh, even for this same purpose have I raised thee up, that I might shew my power in thee, and that my name might be declared throughout all the earth. Therefore hath he mercy on whom he will have mercy, and whom he will he hardeneth (Rom. 9:14–18).

Ever since sin came into the world, man has tried to throw the blame back on God. We remember the story of the fall as recounted in Genesis 3. The woman had sinned ignorantly and the man willfully as the New Testament tells us, and their sin had caused them to flee from God. Their garments of light had disappeared with the coming of sin and they discovered their nakedness—not nakedness which comes from lack of clothing, but nakedness which comes from the loss of righteousness. They had swiftly moved to cover their bodies, but fig leaves were no substitute for light; and when the voice of God came, calling them in the cool of the day, they were afraid and hid themselves.

Ever since that time man has sought to cast the blame for the wrongs that are in this world back on God Himself. The argument of man runs roughly like this: "God has all power and God created everything. Well, if God has all power and if God created everything, isn't He responsible for all that is wrong?" The answer is, "No, He is not responsible; man is responsible."

This is the burden of one of Ezekiel's greatest revelations. Men were crying out against the supposed injustice of God and God answered them in a way that shut their mouths forever. It must be remembered that these instructions were not addressed to the Egyptians or the Philistines, nor to the Romans or the Americans, but that they were addressed to Israel, a people who were in a covenant relationship with God and who had the priesthood, the altar, the atonement, and the promises of God. Some of them had turned back to the ways of sin and, as a result, were existing instead of living. These knew nothing of the tremendous triumph that God has for those who enter into a life of total fulfillment through accepting sovereign grace. They were justified men, but they failed to realize fully that the justified by His faith shall live (Hab. 2:4; Gal. 3:11, etc.). The emphasis is upon the fact that the presence of the new life which God had put within them would bring them out into a life of triumph. In spite of this, they complained that the Lord was unjust. We read, "Yet you say, the way of the Lord is not equal. Hear now, O house of Israel; Is not my way equal? Are not your ways unequal?" (Ezek. 18:25). Since He repeats this, it is best for us to repeat it also. Four verses further along we read, "Yet says the house of Israel, the way of the Lord is not equal. O house of Israel, are not my ways equal? Are not your ways unequal?" (Ezek. 18:29).

God's Word Sufficient

We should understand that God has reasons which are unknown to us. It should be sufficient that we have God's word for it. As I have meditated long upon this section of the Word of God, I have asked the Lord to give me a human illustration that would cover the great revelation of this truth. While all illustrations fall down if expressed in detail, let us imagine a case and compare it with what we have before us here. A small boy has a pet dog which he loves very dearly. He plays with that dog every day and the dog sleeps beside him at night. One day the boy opens the door of the family garage just in time to see his father kill the dog. The fatal shot rings out and the boy screams and rushes toward the dog. The father catches the boy who kicks and screams against him. "You killed my dog. You killed my dog. I hate you. I hate you." The father carries the boy into the house and says, "My son, I will tell you why I had to kill him." But the boy runs from his father, screaming, "I hate you. I hate you. You killed my dog."

In order to make our parable fit the spiritual fact we are trying to explain, we will continue in a somewhat absurd way. Men who act in an absurd way toward God may not see their own absurdity, but they would be quick to detect the absurdity in the parallel. This boy, we will say, continues to live in his father's house, eating the meals that are provided by his father, wearing the clothes that are provided by his father, while constantly saying that he hates his father because his father killed his dog. When the boy grows up and begins to have some understanding of disease, he is given clippings which show that there had been an epidemic of rabies in his neighborhood, that a mad dog had bitten several children, and that some of them had died. He even finds a clipping which states that the mad dog bit several other dogs in the neighborhood and that it was necessary for the owners to destroy those pets. From his maturity the boy can look back on his childhood and see how warped were his opinions of his father. He had carried hatred of his father through the years because his father had crossed his childish will when he was four or five years old. Yet now he sees the evidence that his father was acting in wisdom and love, and that his pet dog might have bitten him and caused his own death.

Rebellious Hearts

It is not necessary to pursue the parallel further. God is the Creator of the universe and our Creator. We stand before Him as creatures. Everything that He does is right and nothing that we do is right unless it is in line with His will for us. He has all knowledge and we have no true knowledge except that which we learn from Him. What Christ said to His disciples in quite another circumstance may be applied to God the Father here at this point. Peter did not want the Lord to wash his feet and Christ had to insist, saying to him, "What I am doing you do not know now, but afterwards you will understand" (John 13:7). The same is true of this doctrine of election. The fact that the Father tells us that He has His reasons for it should be entirely enough for the child. If there are those who hate God because He announces the divine prerogative of choice, it only reveals their own rebellious hearts. As long as we have God's Word for it, that should suffice.

In the development of the thought that now follows, we must continue from the summary of the problem which we have seen to the further unfolding that is now given to us. The choice was in God: Isaac, not Ishmael; Jacob, not Esau. After setting forth these two examples from the book of Genesis, He passes over four hundred years and comes down to Moses at the time of the giving of the law. The people had accepted a covenant of law from God, saying, "All the words which the Lord has said we will do" (Exod. 19:8; 24:3). They had thus bound themselves under the law. When they made a calf of gold and cried, "These be thy gods, O Israel, that brought thee up out of the land of Egypt" (Exod. 32:8), they broke the covenant of law and brought themselves into a place of condemnation. God announced that He would destroy the people. This would have been a righteous act. If they had been destroyed, and if God had made a new people from Moses, as He suggested, God would have been just in so doing. He knew, of course, what He was going to do, but He did it in the way that He did in order to teach the great lesson of His absolute sovereignty. They all deserved death; of that there could be no doubt. If they all perished, they would have perished righteously. It is in just such a framework that God said to Moses, "I will have mercy on whom I will have mercy, and I will have compassion on whom I will have compassion." The words are quoted from the Book of Exodus taken out of a statement made by God on Mount Sinai (Exod. 33:19). The people had been brought to the end of themselves. There was no resource left in man. They were entirely lost. It is then that God announced that He would act for Himself. If we may say so, the doctrine of election was God's secret weapon which made it possible for some men to be saved. If He had not retreated into His sovereignty, as one expositor has described it, there would have been nothing but a curse and no one would have been saved.

Moses asked God if he might be shown the divine glory. God answered, "I will make all my goodness pass before thee and I will proclaim the name of Jehovah before thee; and will be gracious to whom I will be gracious, and will show mercy on whom I will show mercy" (Exod. 33:18, 19).

Grace and Mercy

If at that moment any man had dared to ask for justice, he would have been cut off immediately. The last thing in the world that any man there could have desired was justice. I wish I could convey to you a feeling of the depth of gratitude which I have toward God because I will never have to encounter His justice. I do not want anything to do with the justice of God. I want nothing but His grace, His mercy, His pity, and His compassion. Let me illustrate: Several years ago I was driving the great turnpike across the state of Pennsylvania. The road is wide, straight, and safe. It was a good day. The road was dry. As we drove on hour after hour, my foot grew heavy on the gas. I was not aware of my speed until I saw, beside the road ahead of us, two cars that had drawn off the highway. The situation was unmistakable; there was a state policeman in the act of writing out a ticket to give to another motorist. I glanced at my speed and I saw that I was traveling more than 10 miles per hour above the speed limit. Believe me, I did not want justice at that moment. I took my foot off the accelerator, applied the brakes, and came down within the legal speed limit. As I passed the man who was getting the ticket, I was thankful that I was not having anything to do with justice.

There is no unrighteousness with God. It is unthinkable that there should be injustice in God. The only possible injustice in God would be His failure to punish the sinner for his own sins and His promise to reward some through sheer grace. Grace is not injustice, for it comes to us through the cross of Christ. We shall find, as we continue, that all of man's objections are met and found empty. God assures us that He knows what He is doing, and that He proposes to continue along the lines which He has always used—namely, salvation by grace through faith, apart from anything in the individual who is saved and all upon the undisclosed reasons of His own love locked up in the sovereignty of His own will. Many believers may be startled by Paul's statement "So then it is not of him that willeth nor of him that runneth, but of God that showeth mercy" (Rom. 9:16). Almost all babes in Christ will wonder if their decision did not have something to do with their salvation. Our text sets forth a categorical denial of any such thought. Salvation is not of him that willeth, nor of him that runneth, but of God who showeth mercy. It is not of the willer or of the runner, but of the Pitier. That would be a much closer translation of the Greek. At this point there are two or three proof texts which are generally quoted in an attempt to nullify the plain teaching which is most strongly summarized in the ninth chapter of Romans. It is necessary for us to examine these texts to see what they really mean.

John 1:12, 13

The first of these texts is John 1:12. There we read, "But as many as received him, to them gave he power to become the sons of God even to them that believe on his name." My first answer to those who quote this verse is to ask that the very next verse also be quoted. There we read, "Who were born not of blood, nor of the will of the flesh, nor of the will of man, but of God." I then ask, "Is it proper to use verse 12 to contradict the verse that follows it?" John 1:13 parallels our present text and tells us that the human will is not a factor in the communication of the divine life to a dead soul by Almighty God, the Pitier, who shows mercy upon whom He will. After the divine life has been given to an individual whom God has determined to save, that individual will lift up his head and look to God the Savior. Before the divine life has been communicated to the individual, the individual has no element within him that is capable of a motion toward God. This is what is described as spiritual death. The individual is a combination of mind, emotions, and will. The Bible flatly states that all of these three died in Adam. We have seen how strongly it is stated that the mind can have nothing to do with salvation. In Romans 8:7 we read, "For the carnal mind is enmity against God, for it is not subject to the law of God, neither indeed can be: so then they that are in the flesh cannot please God."

Choosing God

Another type of verse which is frequently quoted in a way to contradict the truth we are now expounding is that which addresses an appeal to one who is already in a covenant relationship with the Lord as though the appeal were addressed to every member of the human race. Someone will say, for example, "But doesn't God say, 'Choose ye this day whom you will serve'" (Josh. 24:15)? The answer to that, of course, is that God did not say to the Egyptians, or the Philistines, or the Greeks, or the Romans that they were to serve, but that He addressed this command to members of His own covenant people, chosen by Him in a special relationship and hedged about with promises and covenants. The people who heard this call had been circumcised, had been divided into tribes, and had the special tribe of Levi as a priesthood in their behalf. There was, for them, the day of the passover in which he blood of sacrificial animals was shed as a sign of the remission of their sins. was, for them, the day of the passover in which the blood of sac-animals was shed for them, even for the sins which they might have committed in ignorance.

There are likewise invitations addressed only to people who are in a covenant relationship with God that are sometimes used by preachers to warn the lost of our day. For example, we may hear someone preach Isaiah's warnings to Israel as though they were warnings to the lost Gentiles in America today. "Let the wicked forsake his way," they will say, "and the unrighteous man his thoughts; and return unto our God, for He will have mercy and abundantly pardon" (Isa. 55:7). The people who were addressed were not the Egyptians or the Hittites of Isaiah's day, but Israelites who were in the covenant and under the covenant promises. The *everyone* to whom he cries in the great invitation, "Ho! Everyone that thirsteth!" cannot remotely be extended to the Ammorites of his day or the Americans of our day. This invitation was given to those of Israel who thirsted. They had already been close to God and were invited to return where they had already been. Such was not the case of the *goyim*, the nations who were, as God tells us, "without Christ, being aliens from the commonwealth of Israel and strangers from the covenants of promise, having no hope, and without God in the world" (Eph. 2:12).

Whosoever Will

At this point in the discussion, someone is sure to demand to know the meaning of the "whosoever will" promises. Here lies the crux of the whole matter. The Bible has many promises that are the equivalent of "whosoever will." We praise God for these great promises. We have already seen from our text that salvation is not of him that willeth nor of him that runneth but of God who shows mercy. Then what is the purpose of the "whosoever will" verses? I believe that they are there in order to vindicate God and to demonstrate that the natural man does not receive the things of the Spirit; that they are foolishness to him (1 Cor. 2:14.) In order that there may be no confusion, because the English word *will* is both an auxiliary verb which denotes future time as well as the verb for volitional choice, let me substitute the word *determine* for this last meaning and say it as "whosoever determines" let him come. "Whosoever will" means "whosoever determines." My next question is: "Who will determine to come to Christ?" The answer from the whole of the Bible is that, by himself, no man will determine to come to Christ. We read at the end of the Bible, "Let him that is athirst come; and whosoever will [whosoever determines], let him take of the water of life freely" (Rev. 22:17). I ask these solemn questions: Who will come? Who will determine? Who will take of the water of life? The answer comes from the whole of the Bible: Nobody, nobody, nobody. Even when Jesus Christ came into the world, He was rejected by His own people Israel and ignored by the Gentiles.

Then why are the promises there? They are there to prove the total depravity of man, to vindicate the righteous judgment of God, and to teach the believer. They teach me, first of all, the abysmal depths of iniquity that was in my heart and show me that I was absolutely incapable if God had not made the first step in my direction. They teach me, in the second place, the wonderful mercy and the unfathomable grace which God has manifested towards us in saving us. He showed us mercy when we did not deserve mercy. He quickened us when we were dead in trespasses and sins. (Eph. 2:1). He made us alive when we were dead. He died for us when we were without strength. (Rom. 5:6). He died for us when we were ungodly sinners (Rom. 5:6, 7). He reconciled us to Himself when we were enemies (Rom. 5:10). In the third place, these verses give me the assurance of eternal life, for if I find myself believing that which the carnal mind cannot believe, receiving that which the natural man cannot receive, loving Him who is the despised and rejected of men; if I find myself hearing His Word and believing on the God who sent Him, then I know I have eternal life. I know that I have been made alive by His Spirit; I know that I have come to Christ because the Father gave me to His Son (John 6:37). I know these things because I find myself doing things which can be done only supernaturally. And I know that the miracle of regeneration is in me.

Finally, some may ask what this does to the doctrine of the freedom of the human will. The Bible's answer is that the will is free for man to choose what he wishes to eat and drink, what he wishes to wear, where he wishes to go, and with whom He wishes to go. The will is free to work or to be lazy, to be charitable or to be miserly. There are ten thousand thousand things which the will is free to do, but in many fields the human will is not free. The old man cannot choose to be young; the sick man cannot choose to be well. The slow man cannot choose to be a champion runner. The moron cannot choose to be intelligent. The world may mark your report card and give you an "A" for effort, but you will still fail in many things because you are simply not able in spite of all your choosing. In all these fields we can see the failure of the human will. Then we enter into the deep mystery of sovereign grace. God Almighty says that when the human race sinned, the will died in that fall so far as any choice about God was concerned. Man could choose to jump off the top of a cliff, but once having jumped, he could no longer choose to avoid the consequences of that great fall. In every part of the Bible, we have the divine revelation that man sinned, that in the sin he fell from God, and that in the fall there was spiritual death. The Lord Jesus Christ said, "No man can come to me except the Father draw him" (John 6:44).

God's Dealings with Pharaoh

As we return to the main channel of our text, we shall see how God will deal in sovereign grace with a Gentile monarch even as He deals in sovereign grace with His own people Israel. God had proclaimed that the seed of His people should be called in Isaac. He had further announced that one of the unborn twins in the womb of their mother would be His beloved Jacob whom He would call Israel, prince with God. In like manner He now reminds His people of what He had said to a Gentile monarch, Pharaoh.

The story of Pharaoh has excited the criticism of many enemies of God's truth. Men do not want God to be sovereign—they wish to have the final decision and control in their own heads and hearts. God has decreed differently and He will ultimately bring to naught any force, power or individual who attempts to vaunt ability, to claim power, or to parade pride. Many of the difficulties which men have found in the story of Pharaoh disappear, however, when we find out what the Bible really teaches.

We must go back to the burning bush where the Lord met Moses and where Moses had to take his shoes off as he stood in God's holy presence (Exod. 3:5). If we have this attitude, we will be able to walk with Moses as he goes toward Egypt. On the road from Midian to Egypt, while Moses was walking in complete obedience to God, "The Lord said to Moses, 'When you go back to Egypt, see that you do before Pharaoh all the miracles which I have put in your power; but I will harden his heart, so that he will not let the people go'" (Exod. 4:21).

Moses went to Pharaoh's palace and delivered God's message to the monarch, requesting the deliverance of the children of Israel from their servitude. This was the order of God. Pharaoh asked to see a miracle and Moses' rod became a serpent before him. I am convinced that Pharaoh knew in his heart that the true God had met Moses and that a wonder had been done before him, but he was looking for a solution that might allow him to have his own way.

CHAPTER V

If God had intervened and performed a miracle of grace upon Pharaoh, his heart would have been softened, and he would have obeyed God. If you ask me why God did not do this, I must reply that I do not know, nor can any man say that he knows why God acts in the way that He does. I am satisfied to rest in the certainty that the Lord knows what He is doing and that He does all things well. Certainly we can see that the result of God's failure to touch the heart of Pharaoh and soften it left it in its hardened condition and allowed it to go on its way of increasing hardness. We can draw from this a tremendous lesson for our own lives, both in the sphere of our actions and our thinking. We must ever take the humble position before God, ever seek to do the will of God, and ever understand that our own will is not the best thing for us if there is in that will any deviation from the perfect will of God. Constantly we must turn to the Word of God to know His will in order that we may be obedient to it. Our prayer must be the prayer of David when he cried, "Search me, Oh God, and know my heart! Try me and know my thoughts! See if there be any wicked way in me and lead me in the way everlasting" (Ps. 139:23, 24).

VI

The Children of Sovereignty

You will say to me then, "Why does he still find fault?" For who can resist his will?" But, who are you, a man, to answer back to God? Shall the thing formed say to Him that formed it, "Why have you made me thus?" Has the potter no right over the clay, to make out of the same lump one vessel for beauty and another for menial use? What if God, desiring to show His wrath and to make known His power, has endured with much patience the vessels of wrath made for destruction, in order to make known the riches of His glory for the vessels of mercy, which He has prepared beforehand for glory, even us whom He has called, not from the Jews only, but also from the Gentiles? As indeed He says in Hosea, "Those who were not my people I will call 'my people,' and her who was not beloved I will call 'my beloved.'" "And in the very place where it was said to them, 'You are not my people,' they will be called 'sons of the living God.'" And Isaiah cries out concerning Israel: "Though the number of the sons of Israel be as the sand of the sea, only a remnant of them will be saved; for the Lord will execute his sentence upon the earth with rigor and dispatch." And as Isaiah predicted, "If the Lord of hosts had not left us children, we would have fared like Sodom and been made like Gomorrah." What shall we say, then? That Gentiles who did not pursue righteousness have attained it, that is, righteousness through faith; but that Israel who pursued the righteousness which is based on law did not succeed in fulfilling that law. Why? Because they did not pursue it through faith, but as if it were based on works. They have stumbled over the stumbling stone, as it is written, "Behold I am laying in Zion a stone that will make men stumble, a rock that will make them fall; and he who believes in him will not be put to shame" (Rom. 9:19–33).

There can be no doubt of the impression that Paul's teaching had made on his opponents. The questions that they raised show the nature of his teaching. In his

CHAPTER VI

usual fashion, which we have seen so many times before, he takes the question that they have formed, boldly states it, and boldly answers it.

God's Responsibility

The studies that we have pursued through the preceeding verses show us that men are in a lost condition and that nobody could have been saved if God had not moved to save some by His grace. Logically, at this point we might be moved to echo the question which was put to Paul: "If salvation is by the will of God, then why does God find fault if some are not saved, if they could have been if he had been pleased to quicken them as he did those whom he chose to make alive in Christ?" The question is a loaded one because it implies that God is responsible for man's lost condition. The Bible definitely teaches the contrary. Men are not lost because God has not chosen them to be saved; men are lost simply because they have rebelled against the light and truth which God has given them. "And this is the condemnation, that the light has come into the world, and men love darkness rather than light, because their deeds are evil, for everyone who does evil hates the light and does not come to the light lest his deeds should be exposed. But he who does what is true comes to the light, that it may be clearly seen that his deeds have been wrought in God" (John 3:19–21). God assures us that the light of which He speaks was not given to a special class. "That was the true Light which lighted *every man* that cometh into the world. He was in the world, and the world was made by him, and the world ignored him. He came to his own people and his own people rejected him" (John 1:9–11). Men were not ignorant of the truth; they were in rebellion against it. "For the wrath of God is revealed from heaven against all ungodliness and unrighteousness of men *who hold the truth in unrighteousness*;" (Rom. 1:18). Again, "and even as they did not like to retain God in their knowledge, God gave them over to a reprobate mind, to do those things which are not proper" (Rom. 1:28). Thus, in answer to the question: "Why does God find fault?", He replies that He finds fault because men are at fault; they are in rebellion against Him. Men are not ignorant of His Word, neither are they helpless to obey it, but they are in outright rebellion against it.

Having answered boldly their questions, the Apostle Paul now speaks against the spirit that animated it. This spirit wishes to exalt man to a place of equality with God, or even superiority. Man wishes to be consulted or to have his mind sit in judgment on the plans of God. God reminds them that they are creatures and that He is the Creator. There are some who storm at this and answer that there is not sufficient reason given. We realize, of course, that God could have given much more reason than that which is set forth here, but God has given us all that we need to know and all that our little minds can take in.

God alone is wisdom; God alone is right. God alone can make the decisions. There is no power or might or wisdom or justice apart from God. Shall a man therefore, answer back to God? Shall the things formed say to Him that formed them, "Why have you made me thus?"

Sovereign of Creation

Years ago, when I was living in France, I knew a potter who had a small pottery shop in which he made various types of vessels for all sorts of uses. Often I went to watch him turning the wheel and molding the various vessels according to his desire. At times he let me take a lump of clay and work awkwardly at the craft that he did so beautifully. I had been reading the great passages in Isaiah and Jeremiah which have to do with the prophets' visit to the house of a potter and the illustrations which grew out of that craft. I asked the potter one day, when he had taken a lump of clay and put it upon his wheel, what determined his choice as to what he should make. I saw him make tableware, kitchenware, and small pots. He said that he got the feel of it as he began to work. When he was rested, he made beautiful things; when he was tired, he would slap the clay on the wheel and turn out ordinary vessels which sold in the market for menial purposes. He put clay on his wheel and I asked him to make a menial vessel. He tossed one off in a moment. I then asked him to make a vase, and with great care and love he made a vessel of beauty. I asked him if he ever switched from one object to another while he was in the midst of the work. He began again and speedily there arose before my eyes a vase. While the clay was still wet and whirling, he struck it from above with a heavy sweep of his hand, crushed it to a lump, and speedily ran up the form of another vessel. Moment after moment I saw various forms succeeding each other as he desired—all from the same lump of clay. With a deft touch, there appeared a bowl, a plate, a cup, or a dish. He was absolutely master of his clay.

God sets before us here in our text that He is the absolute master of His creation. He does not work by whim, nor is He ever tired so that He shifts to another pattern. He wants us to recognize that he has his purposes which are right according to all that He is in His inward nature so that our hope and trust might be in Him alone.

Man has dared to criticize God as though God were not sovereign. The Holy Spirit has shown through the Word that God is sovereign. He also describes the way God has been acting in His sovereign patience through the centuries. "What if God, desiring to make known his power, has endured with much patience the vessels of wrath fitted for destruction, in order to make known the riches of his glory . . . ?" We have only to look back through history and know how true this declaration is. The absolute authority of God over His creatures has been so manifested that no honest man could fairly dispute it. This absolute authority was never used by God in any arbitrary fashion, but always with "much long-suffering."

God's Treatment of Adam

Was God arbitrary with Adam when sin first entered the human race? Was God hasty in bringing heavy penalties upon man? Were Adam and Eve flung off into hell so that God could begin again with another creation, or was He full of love and compassion toward these erring ones? One of the most touching lines in all of the Bible is the question that came from the loving voice of God after man had sinned: "Adam, where art thou?" (Gen. 3:9). God knew, of course, where Adam was and could have appeared before the puny sinners in the brightness of His majesty. Instead, knowing that sin had brought fright to Adam, God sent on ahead the sound of a voice only, giving time, as it were, for man to calm his agitation and be prepared for the judgment scene which followed. Before any word of judgment was pronounced against the man, the loving God prepared the way by announcing more dire judgment against Satan. In the course of that judgment, He found a way to comfort man in advance of judgment by incorporating into it the first promise of the Gospel.

Throughout the Bible there is the record of God's patience with those whom we know to be objects of His complete salvation; but when we look at those who we know have acted as His enemies to the end, we find the same patient endurance. Long-suffering is one of the loveliest attributes of God. Indeed, God was so patient with the wicked that there were times when it seemed that He was condoning sin. This charge would still lie against God if He had not vindicated His righteousness by coming forth to die in Jesus Christ, that He, Himself, might be just and the justifier of him that believes in Jesus. (Rom. 3:26) No, His patience must not be considered as indifference to evil or any thought of fellowship with it. Rather, we must see that the history of all nations, when judged by centuries and not by generations, not only shows that God loved righteousness and hated iniquity but that He was always "slow to anger and plenteous in mercy" (Ps. 86:15). A thousand times, yes thousands upon thousands of times, men have turned flowering fields into fields of blood and the most brutal have exercised their craft not only against fellow men but in their minds, they have also warred against God. His patience toward them did not cure their hatred, but rather incited them the more to war against Him. "The carnal mind is enmity against God" (Rom. 8:7), and "when we were enemies" (Rom. 5:10), patience rose to its highest in presenting love and grace.

Pharaoh

Let us return for a moment to the man in the Bible who is the subtle illustration of our paragraph in Romans. "What if God, desiring to show his wrath and to make known his power, has endured with patience, Pharaoh as a vessel of wrath who had fitted himself for destruction?" If God had pleased, He might have cut off Pharaoh on his first refusal to let the people of Israel go; or at any one of the ten successive plagues, but God was not *obliged* to do so. He was surely at liberty to spare him, exercise forbearance toward him, to remove in succession the different plagues from him, and to give him space for repentance until he had filled up the measure of his iniquities and was quite ripe for those signal judgments that had been pronounced against him.

The Golden Calf

In like manner, the nation of Israel might justly have been cut off when they renounced their allegiance to God and worshipped the golden calf. God might, without any impeachment of His justice, have executed the threatened judgment of destroying instantly that rebellious nation and raising up another from the loins of Moses. But He saw fit to exercise mercy toward them and to impart to them yet more abundant communications of His grace and favor. Surely in this He did them no injury. So also, under all their provocations in the wilderness during the space of forty years, and under all their apostasies from Him in the land of Canaan for the space of fifteen hundred years, He might, if He had seen fit, have destroyed them: To say the least, He did them no injury in bearing with them until, by the crucifixion of their Messiah, they had "filled up the measure of their own and their fathers' iniquities." God's foreknowledge of how much they would abuse His mercies was no reason why He should not exercise mercy toward them. By His patience and forbearance, His mercy was displayed; and by their accumulated guilt and aggravated condemnation, His indignation against sin and His power to avenge it were the more conspicuously displayed. We may say the same in reference to any person or number of persons; God is not bound to cut them off the moment they sin against Him; He may continue to cultivate the barren fig tree year after year, if He be so pleased, in order to show more clearly its incurable sterility.

God's Dealing with His Children

So also He may pursue a similar line of conduct toward the vessels of mercy, in order ultimately to "make known upon them the riches of His glory." God was not compelled to bring Abraham out from his family and his country while he was yet a child. God was at liberty to leave him (as He did) bowing down to sticks and stones like all the rest around him, until the hour had arrived which He in His secret counsel had appointed for His effectual calling. Nor, when God called Abraham, was He compelled to call other Gentiles at the same time. He was at liberty to leave them to their own ways until the time of the Messiah in order to show more fully that "the world by wisdom knew not God," and that, if left to themselves, nothing but universal ruin would follow.

When we consider the life of Paul, we have the same truth illustrated. Paul tells us, twice, that God had separated him as a chosen vessel even from his mother's womb. Yet, in spite of this, God left him for many years to his own ways, even to the committing of murder. Was God unjust in this? Was there any obligation binding God to Paul earlier than He did? Was not God free to allow Paul to go on, deceived, until the enormity of his conduct could furnish a more solid contrast to the grace of God which becomes more glorious when we see it exercised in such a way, on such a man, and at such a time? Consider also the thief whom God saved when he was dying beside Christ on the cross. Certainly God was at liberty to allow him to continue in his course of robbery and murder up to the very last hour of his life, in order that He might show, even in the moment of dying, that grace could come to the worst of sinners at the eleventh hour in their life span if God so desired it. In acting as He acted, God did not injure those whom He thus blessed, nor did He injure those whom He did not save; they were already in the provision for which they had fitted themselves. If God had not saved Abraham, Paul, or the thief on the cross, He would certainly not have done them any injustice, for they deserved nothing of Him.

God allowed misery and sin and death to proceed on their terrible way in order that when He moved to deliver someone from them, His own grace and power might shine forth all the more brightly. Thus it was that Christ, though He had the power to heal Lazarus at a distance, allowed him to sicken and die, and allowed his body to be corrupted for four days. He did this on purpose so that His own power might be the more abundantly visible and glorious.

The Children of Sovereignty

No Credit Due Us

Since those of us who are saved are called vessels of mercy prepared for glory by God, we can take none of the credit for anything that is ours. In our salvation we have become the objects of a new creation (2 Cor. 5:17). The potter has taken new clay from the divine lump and has made us partakers of His own divine nature. I have wondered how I could illustrate this truth so that we could visualize what it is that God has done for us. Those who have seen training films made by the cartoon method can perhaps understand the following: A large bowl stands in the center of the picture; the bowl is broken into a hundred pieces and the pieces can be seen falling down—but at the same time, the cartoonist leaves a dotted line to show the form of the bowl as it was before it was broken. Suddenly, even though the old pieces lie around in confusion, a new bowl that cannot be broken is poured into the old outline. None of the old pieces are used in the creation of the new bowl. Finally, the old pieces are swept away and nothing but the new bowl remains. This is what really happens to men who are saved. We are bowls of wrath since we have the power to break ourselves and not have the power to put ourselves back together again. God is not going to be frustrated by man's wilfulness and sin. He determines to pour new life into our molds. In His own time and in His own way, both unknown to us, he quickens us and makes us alive in Christ. At first all that those around can see is nothing more than the fragments of the old Adamic nature, which do not diffier fundamentally from the fragments in any other human being. Little by little, the presence of the divine nature begins to make itself manifest. We are changed from glory to glory by the presence of the Holy Spirit who is now come to dwell within. (2 Cor. 3:18) From the moment we are saved, we look forward to the future, rejoicing in the hope of the glory of God (Rom. 5:2). The glory which God gave to the risen Lord Jesus Christ is transferred to our account. (1 Peter 1:21; John 17:22) Thus, while we continue living here on this earth, we are looking forward to the glory that shall be revealed in us, reckoning that the sufferings of this present time are nothing in comparison to that which lies before us (Rom. 8:18).

The Gentiles

Throughout this chapter, the argument has been an answer to those who held that God could not bless Gentiles because He committed Himself to Abraham. The answer has been that the same causes, hidden in God Himself, that moved Him to choose Abraham rather than some Egyptian or Babylonian, Isaac rather than Ishmael, and Jacob rather than Esau, were still operating in all of His choices. He was sovereign and worked always according to the good pleasure of His holy will.

Amazingly enough, what He was now doing for the Gentiles, He had caused to be written down in the ancient prophecies. The verses were there in Hosea and Isaiah for all to read. The selfish blindness of people grown hard in the pride of their own self-righteousness had made it impossible for them to read truth where it was written—but written it was and nothing could change it.

The ancient oracles of the demon gods used vague phrases that might have many crude interpretations. The Word of God was nothing like this; the prophecies were so definite and so un mistakable that it was impossible to gainsay them. Nevertheless, in the midst of words which made definite commitments to Israel, there were hidden promises which must also be applied to the Gentiles. God had made His commitments, but He had reserved to Himself the right to go beyond and make other commitments.

Hosea's Children

Let us look first at the prophecy in Hosea in its primary meaning. Hosea had been called upon by God to perform the most difficult task ever committed to one of the prophets—He was to marry a harlot in order to act out a pageant of love linked to unfaithfulness. Hosea would represent God and the wife would represent Israel, the faithless one. We have already seen this story as it relates to the relationship between the husband and the wife. We now see it as it refers to the teaching that was given by the names of the children. Names in the Old Testament are highly significant and those in the early part of Hosea are especially so. The children that were born were named by God Himself. The first child was named Jezreel, the second child was named Lo-Ruhamah, and the third child was named Lo-Ammi. Before the story was done, the names were changed to names of grace, but first the names of woe had to be written and the long fulfillment had to run its weary course.

Jezreel is a Hebrew word that describes the action when the human hand grasps an object and throws it away. There was a valley that went by this name. Jehu had exterminated the family of Ahab there and had taken the power over Israel. He did not do that which was right in the sight of the Lord and God announced that the power over Israel would depart from his house in the fourth generation and that this would take place in the valley of Jezreel. (2 Kings 10:30, 31) It was as though a Spanish child had been named Armada half a century before the power of Spain was broken in the defeat of the Armada. To name this child Jezreel was the announcement by God that He would scatter the children of Israel as a man takes a handful of litter and throws it to the wind. How terribly that prophecy has been fulfilled is illustrated in the fact that the children of Israel today are scattered to the uttermost parts of the earth.

The second child was named Lo-Ruhamah which means "unpitied." It was the announcement by God that the day would come when the children of Israel would have no pity from Him. How terribly that prophecy has been fulfilled we can see even in the history of our own generation. The pogroms of Poland and the concentration camps of Germany are filled with stories of the ruthless destruction of the descendants of God's ancient people. Dachau and Belsen-Bergen have become names of infamy where Gentiles worried the harried people and where their tears of blood brought no pity to the eyes of their captors. In all the history of the world there has been no more frightful chapter written, and it was all described more than two thousand seven hundred years before the event.

The third child was named Lo-Ammi which means simply "not-my-people." Hosea heard the terrible word, "Call his name Lo-Ammi: for you are not my people, and I will not be your God" (Hosea 1:9). Sad as it is to write these words, they must be written here in this twentieth century because we are still living in the days of this prophecy. Never has so much been said in so few words. When Churchill wrote his memoirs, he found admirable phrases well-suited to be the titles of the volumes describing the events they covered, such as: *Their Finest Hour* and *The Hinge of Fate*. If someone had written a three-volume history of the Jews, it would have been impossible to find titles more exactly describing these last three thousand years of their history: Jezreel, Lo-Ruhamah, Lo-Ammi—scattered, not pitied, and not my people.

The prophecy continues and God announces that the names of the children shall yet be changed. In the Hebrew manuscripts there is not so much as an extra space between the letters that end the prophecy of judgment and those that jump centuries to tell of the promises of blessing. Suddenly the tone turns from despair to triumph and we read, "Yet the number of the children of Israel shall be as the sand of the sea which cannot be measured nor numbered; then it shall come to pass, that in the place where it was said to them, you are not my people, it shall be said unto them, you are the sons of the living God. Then shall the children of Judah and the children of Israel be gathered together, and appoint themselves one head, and they shall come up out of the land; for great shall be the day of Jezreel. Say unto your brethren, 'Ammi,' and to your sisters, 'Ruhamah'" (Hosea 1:10, 11; 2:1).

Just as *Jezreel* is the Hebrew word that describes the action when the human hand grasps an object and throws it away, even so the same word is that which describes the action when the sower takes a handful of grain and plants it for the new harvest. Thus, the name of the first child was changed by God from *Scattered* to *Planted*, and that of the second child from *Not Pitied* to *Pitied*, and that of the third child from *Not-My-People* to *My People*.

CHAPTER VI

We can well understand that Satan hates this and similar prophecies. That God should be faithful to a faithless people is the revelation of grace which is the heart of the Gospel. That this grace was made possible by God's coming in Christ to die and to provide redemption for lost men is the defeat of Satan and also the just grounds for his condemnation. In all centuries, therefore, anti-Semitism has been one of the vilest of sins because it is a rebellion against the sovereign God. Racial hatred of any kind is despicable; that which exists between Turk and Greek, between Hindu and Moslem is selfish, proud, and hateful. That which exists against the Jew is not only a sin against man, it is a sin against Deity.

Grace Alone

In the ninth chapter of Romans, the main theme is not the eventual blessing of Israel but the present blessing of Israel and Gentile alike, as individuals are called out of both groups to form the body of believers that is the true Church. Suddenly the wonder of the prophecy breaks forth. God had planned for a group that should be more than governmental subjects. Israel was a chosen people, an elect nation; the Church was to be made up of a company of sons. The title that is now ours in Christ is that which has been announced prophetically—sons of the living God. What wonderful grace is here! Once we were bearers of other names, names of horror. We were *goyim*, Gentiles, who were called dogs even by the Lord Jesus Christ. We were "the uncircumcision," and when the name is used of Gentiles in the New Testament, there is the lash of scorn to be found in it. (Eph. 2:11) Before Christ came, we were "without Christ, being aliens from the commonwealth of Israel and strangers from the covenants of promise, having no hope without God in the world" (Eph. 2:12). Christless, hopeless, and godless! What expressions could better convey the horror of the natural Gentile position? Then Christ dies and grace is seen overflowing. Those who were once outside as unclean dogs are now "the sons of the living God."

Then, almost suddenly, the apostle quotes two verses from Isaiah which take us down through the future to the end of Israel's history. At the time of Paul, the nation had been set aside and God counted the fulfillment of His promises in a feeble remnant of which Paul was an outstanding member. The people who were objecting to the grace of God for Gentiles had to know that though their number became as the sand of the sea, God would not be bound to do anything for the whole of the nation simply because they thought they had a patent and a copyright on God. The remnant of them will be saved.

This principle of God's sovereign choice having been established, the conclusion is now evident. God declares that men are saved entirely by God Himself and that the only thing a man can do in order to be saved is simply to believe that he cannot be saved by himself, and therefore turn to accept the fact that what God did in Christ is all that matters.

Now this is that which is set forth in the last paragraph of our chapter. Paul compares the two attitudes of men who look toward heaven. Some look and decide that they must get there by trying. Others, knowing that they can never get there by trying, take salvation in the simplicity with which God has given it to us.

In reading this paragraph again, we must note an important correction in the translation. The King James Version has made a mistake here which could mislead an individual. We read that the Gentiles who followed not after righteousness have attained to righteousness, even the righteousness which is of faith; but Israel, which followed after the law of righteousness, has not attained to the law of righteousness. What I call your attention to is the use of the word *attained*. The KJV says the Gentiles attained and that Israel has not attained. In the English it is the same word, but in the Greek there are two very different words: *katalambano* and *phthano*. Perhaps I can illustrate the difference by telling a story. Some time ago I saw a cartoon in one of our national magazines. It showed a scene in the board room of some industrial company where the president of the company was standing before his subordinates. On the wall behind him was a portrait of a man dressed in the style of the previous generation, who by the likeness was most evidently his father, the founder of the business. The president was scowling fiercely and saying to his salesmen, "The trouble with you men is that you have no initiative. Why, by the time I was thirty years old, I had *inherited* my first five million dollars." Well, believe me, there is a big difference between inheriting five million dollars and earning five million dollars. The two Greek words here set forth that difference. Our KJV says that the Gentiles attained righteousness and Israel did not attain to the law of righteousness. The Gentiles who followed not after righteousness, suddenly inherited, obtained, or received the free gift of life in Christ by grace through faith. The people of Israel who tried to earn it, did not get it.

The Stumbling Stone

The chapter concludes with one more question and a simple explanation. After stating that the Gentile believers had obtained, inherited, or received the righteousness which is of faith, the Bible states that Israel, which followed after the law of righteousness, did not get it or did not reach it. There comes the sharp question, "Why not?" A simple answer is given: "Because they did not look for it in the way of faith but hunted for it in the direction of the works of the law." We might paraphrase this: Because they would not take it on God's easy way, but insisted on trying to do it for themselves.

CHAPTER VI

The heart rebels against being told that it is in a position where it can do nothing for itself, indeed, that anything that it seeks to do only takes it farther away from God. This, God reveals, is a stumbling block over which men trip and fall, even into outer darkness forever.

In the beginning of man's history, God placed a symbol before man as a sign of man's dependence upon God. It was the forbidden fruit of the tree of the knowledge of good and evil. This is not the place to discuss the nature of that tree or that fruit. Suffice it to say that it was a symbol of the fact that man was a creature and that God is the Creator. Man, in keeping his hands off the fruit, would declare that he acknowledged his utter dependence on God. Man, in taking that fruit, declared his independence of God. From this independence, which, of course, is not real but only fancy, come all of the ills of man.

Finally, it should be noted that God transfers the figure of the stumbling stone from an idea to the person of Christ. Why do some men not reach the righteousness of God? Because they tripped over the stumbling stone of the simplicity of the idea of getting it for nothing but the grace of God. This stumbling stone is nothing more or less than salvation through the Lord Jesus Christ and through Him alone. "As it is written, behold I lay in Zion a stumbling stone and a rock of offense; and whosoever believeth in him shall not be ashamed."

Christ is the stumbling stone. This is an astonishing figure of speech until we look at it closely. Then we realize how God presents Christ to us, and how that presentation offends everything that is in the natural heart. Men are willing to accept a Jesus of their own description, but they refuse the Lord Jesus Christ of the Bible. The Christ of the Bible is the Christ of the cross. The Christ of the Bible is not a man giving men an example but He is God coming to die as the Savior. The Christ of the Bible is not the Christ of ethics that men are to have as their goal but the Christ of death and risen life, the Christ who furnishes an absolutely new life which is the only life that is acceptable to God. It is not necessary to give up anything in the world in order to accept another Jesus of human imagination; it is necessary to become spiritually bankrupt before we can come to the Christ of the Bible. Our old Adam can think positively about a human Jesus and still retain some self-respect; when we come to the Christ of the cross, we must think negatively and begin by losing every vestige of confidence or respect for man's original nature. This is why the Lord Jesus Christ is characterized as a stone of stumbling and a rock of offense.

VII

Righteousness—The False and the True

Brethren, my heart's desire and prayer to God for Israel is, that they might be saved. For I bear them record that they have a zeal of God, but not according to knowledge. For they being ignorant of God's righteousness, and going about to establish their own righteousness, have not submitted themselves unto the righteousness of God (Rom. 10:1–3).

With the tenth chapter, the epistle to the Romans moves on in its triumphant logic, bringing us ever farther into the plan of God. The opening verse is astonishing in view of what has just been written. The ninth chapter tells us of Israel's unbelief and of God's expansion of His plan to bring Gentiles unto salvation. At the moment when it appears that Israel's sin has brought the nation under such condemnation that there is no future for her, Paul's heart throbs on in a great revelation of love and hope for his people. He cries out, "Oh for their salvation, brothers! That is my heart's desire and prayer to God." Contrast this for a moment with the beginning of the preceeding chapter. There Paul pours out the expression of his heart's grief for his people. Here he is pouring out the expression of his love. If either of these emotions is real, the other one must be also. We cannot have love for people if we do not grieve because of any sinfulness in them which separates them from the blessing which God can give in fullness only to those who are in His will. If we have grief because of any wrong that we see, there must follow a love which seeks to bring the erring ones into touch with the only source of pardon and blessing. It is this marriage of grief and love which shows the heart of the Christian who is yielded to the Lord and who is seeking to be as Christ in the world, loving men and drawing them back to God.

CHAPTER VII

Paul's people after the flesh, on the whole, have rejected the Lord Jesus Christ. He groans because of this, but his prayer and his cry seem to indicate that there is yet much hope. If only they can be brought to see the true nature of salvation, perhaps they can be made to turn from themselves and be led back to the grace of God. Paul could bear them record that they had a zeal of God, but not according to knowledge. The religious leaders in Paul's day were in the terrible state of having a powerful force of zeal that was not channeled. The result was that it tore the nation to pieces and, like a flood of water that has gone beyond the banks, acted as a destructive force. Ignorance of God and His ways removes all constraint and allows these emotional forces to rage unchecked. That which destroyed Israel in the days of Paul is the same force that destroys nations and individual men in our day. It is the same force which causes men to establish their own righteousness contrary to the righteousness which God has revealed in His Word.

Righteousness

Man has an idea of righteousness that is completely alien from the idea of righteousness which is held by God. Here we have the declaration that human righteousness is not the same kind as divine righteousness. There are those who believe that the matter of righteousness is to be defined and studied according to human conduct. The normal must be found in the lives of men. There are some who are called "good", others who are called "bad", and still others who might be called "better" or "worse" because of various actions which they have performed. There have been many people who have attempted to describe in a study of ethics the various levels of righteousness, continuing from the thoughts and deed of the most depraved on to the most saintly of human beings. Then they have passed from there to thinking that the righteousness of God is something that is to be studied in the same context as human righteousness. They will consent to the fact that there is a gap, even a large gap, between the best of men and God, but they think that there are men who are a long way toward the achievement of a righteousness which can be compared with the righteousness of God.

But God declares throughout the whole of Scripture that His righteousness is not to be considered in the same category as human righteousness. It is unfortunate that the same vocabulary had to be used to describe both the good actions of men and the holy actions of God. As long as we understand that man's righteousness and God's righteousness are different, not in degree but in kind, we can come out at the right end of our discussion. Let us examine man's righteousness at its source and then examine God's righteousness at its source.

This will largely resolve the problem. Man's righteousness is not that which Adam possessed when he was created by God. Man's righteousness is that which man has evolved since he turned away in rebellion against God. The source of man's righteousness is in the sinful nature and being of man.

Many years ago, I published a little paragraph in our magazine and had it illustrated with one or two of the little dolls that are made with a half sphere of lead in the base so that they will always swing upright no matter how they are placed. Stand them on their head and they will almost leap to turn over. Lay them down flat and they will come to the upright position immediately. I used the story to state that the Christian will always triumph over his circumstances when he is solidly established in Jesus Christ. Today I want to go back to those same dolls, but with a new application of this story because I have seen one of these dolls, fashioned like a clown, but with a large lead-filled head so that the clown is always standing upside down. Place him upright on his pointed feet and he will immediately turn over and stand on his head. This is the true picture of the human race since sin entered the heart of mankind. Man looks at everything in his universe from a distorted position. Man's whole world is upside down. The Bible says that man can neither think straight nor understand correctly. "The natural man receiveth not the things of the spirit; they are foolishness unto him, neither can he know them; they are spiritually discerned." (1 Cor. 2:14) When a man is born again, transformed by the power and grace of God through the Lord Jesus Christ, a change takes place in him as definite as though the lead were removed from the head of the clown and put into his feet so that he could stand upright and only upright, instead of being on his head. "If any man be in Christ he is a new creation; old things have passed away and all things are become new" (2 Cor. 5:17).

The man who has not passed through Christ will always have the distorted thoughts that are an intrinsic part of the human race, that are as much a part of the human race as such physical characteristics as having two arms, two legs, and one head. His righteousness will be a social quality which he will have established as a way whereby men can live with one another when each man wants to be the center of all life and to consider all things first of all in a relationship to himself. He cannot think otherwise, for that is the nature of his being.

The righteousness of God, however, has its source in the being of God. It is more than a part of His being. It is God's very self. He is righteousness just as He is love. The righteousness of God is not something He has worked out as a method whereby He can get along with other creatures. He is the Creator and there is none like unto Him. The righteousness of God is perfected without thought of degree. With Him is no variation due to change or due to a shadow of turning (Jas. 1:17). Because He is love and manifests Himself in grace, there is never anything in Him that we can call selfish by human definition. His motives are always for the best of all of His creatures; and if those creatures would abandon their own desires and submit to Him, they would always have that which is best for them. Unfortunately, they do not recognize this fact and, therefore, they are in a state of great frustration. Men want what they think is good and they rush around madly trying to get it. They never attain that for which they are reaching and they never arrive at the goals which they set for themselves.

Being ignorant of God's righteousness, they go about to establish their own righteousness. In other words, they attempt to claim that human righteousness is good, that it is satisfactory, and that because it is satisfactory to men, God should also be satisfied with that righteousness. When this claim is examined, it is seen to be a subtle part of the rebellion that began when man struck out on his own. Ultimately it is also the rejection of God's manifestation in the Lord Jesus Christ.

Christ Our Righteousness

Christ crucified is the righteousness of God. This is the righteousness of which Israel was ignorant. This is the righteousness which they rejected. This is the righteousness against which they erected a system of their own private righteousness in order that they might not have to bow before Christ as the righteousness of God. This is the righteousness against which all the legalists of our own days are arrayed. The fact that Israel was ignorant of this righteousness was not because of any defect in the knowledge which had been set before them. The proclamation of the Gospel which they had heard from the day of Pentecost was in complete harmony with their own prophets and was the fulfillment and confirmation of their prophecies.

What grieved Paul most was his realization of the fact that their present religious position was the result of a hardness of heart that came from the rejection of truth. This hardness was the thing that caused them to cling all the more tightly to their human religion of form and ceremony and to reject all that was central in the revelation that God had given their fathers in the redemption that He had now revealed to them. They had rejected all that was in Christ and thus were left to their own devices which would bring their final condemnation. In the Proverbs we have the inspired word, "There is more hope for a fool than for a man who is wise in his own eyes" (Prov. 26:12). The reason the nation rejected the Lord Jesus at the time of His appearance on earth was their ignorance of the method by which God makes men righteous. Being ignorant of this fact implies ignorance of the character of God, ignorance of the requirement of the law, and ignorance of our own sinful nature.

The first definition of the righteousness of God is that it describes the holiness of God. In our text, it cannot mean that those who were ignorant of the holiness of God established their own moral excellence and so failed to submit themselves to the holiness of God. The second definition is that it refers to the method of justification which God has established. The third definition is that it refers to the righteousness of which God is the author, the righteousness of which He approves and which He accepts.

Personally, I would roll all three of these into one definition and say, with the next verse, that the righteousness of God is none other than the Lord Jesus Christ. When we have said that the divine righteousness is the Lord Jesus Christ, we have seen the holiness of God; we have seen the way whereby God saves men, and we have seen the righteousness which He is and which He bestows and imparts to those who are made alive in Christ.

If we read our verse this way, it can be paraphrased: "They, being ignorant of the Lord Jesus Christ and going about to establish some other method of acceptance and approach to God, have not submitted themselves to the Lord Jesus Christ."

No Submission

Did Israel understand any of this? Our text tells us that they did not submit to the righteousness of God that was manifest in Jesus Christ. He was not only the head of the Church; He was also the head of Israel. As Israel's head, He had to drink with them and for them those bitter sufferings that befall that nation here as well as to die that death which was due to His people. Christ was the holy Suffering One; He was the Holy One; yet, at the same time He was saying, "Mine iniquities... are more (in number) than the hairs on mine head" (Ps. 40:12). When Israel saw this, did they understand it? Did they thank God that He had sent this great sufferer—one who was not only suffering for them but, in the midst of all those sufferings, was presenting His own perfect holiness as a sacrifice to God on their behalf? There was always this duplicate character in Christ; His righteousness was manifested in the suffering. It was under the weight of suffering that the perfectness of the Holy One was manifested. Thus it was that Jesus presented the sweet-smelling savor of His own righteousness to God the Father. It was proved righteousness, tried righteousness, righteousness exercised in many and varied forms of suffering, and at last it was righteousness exercised under the very depths of the wrath of God. It was pure, fragrant righteousness, always acceptable as the frankincense that ascended before God. Why was this righteousness presented?

CHAPTER VII

So that it might be accepted by God for His people. Thus, there were these two things in the sacrifice of Christ: righteousness and suffering.

Because it was all done in suffering and not in glory, because it was something that seemed to bring Him so very low—as He had said in the Psalm to which we have referred, "I am a worm and no man; thou hast brought me into the dust of death!"—because they saw this, they despised it and they despised Him. They would not have despised exalted humanity or a divine humanity, but this true humanity—glory and suffering humanity—they despised utterly.

Rejection of Christ

The first reason for the rejection of Christ was that which they saw in Him. The second reason for the rejection was for all that was in Him which they did not see. When all the righteousness which Jesus Christ was and which He performed was presented to Israel as being what is called here, God's righteousness, they rejected Him. Think of all that can be seen in that phrase: God's righteousness, a righteousness prepared by God, a righteousness that God in the Gospel holds in His hand and presents to each of His believing people. In every sense, it is the righteousness of God. Christ was presented to His people as "the Lord our righteousness." (Jer. 23:6; 33:16). He was the righteousness of every believing Israelite and, after His death, the righteousness of every believing Gentile. "In the Lord shall all the seed of Israel be justified, and shall glory" (Isa. 45:25). But they spurned Him. They were going about to establish a righteousness of their own and refused to submit themselves.

Here, perhaps, is the core of all rejection. Men do not want to submit. The Greek word for submit is found 39 times in the New Testament. It is translated in ways which show its inner meaning of bringing the whole being into subjection to Christ, even as all things one day shall be brought in subjection to Him. Men say that they cannot believe; God says they will not believe. The root meaning of surrender is to hand over one's self. If we are not to be ignorant of God's righteousness, if we are to turn away from any attempt to establish our own righteousness; we must come to the place where we submit ourselves to the righteousness of God as it is seen in the lowliness of the Lord Jesus Christ, as it is seen in the crushing and scorching of His humanity in suffering, and as it is seen on the cross displaying the grace of God which makes it possible for that righteousness to be given us today.

VIII

The Righteousness of Faith

For Christ is the end of the law for righteousness to every one that believeth. For Moses describeth the righteousness which is of the law. That the man which doeth those things shall live by them. But the righteousness which is of faith speaketh on this wise, Say not in thine heart, Who shall ascend into heaven? (that is, to bring Christ down from above:) Or, Who shall descend into the deep? (that is, to bring up Christ again from the dead.) But what saith it? The word is nigh thee, even in thy mouth, and in thy heart: that is, the word of faith, which we preach; That if thou shalt confess with thy mouth the Lord Jesus, and shalt believe in thine heart that God hath raised him from the dead, thou shalt be saved. For with the heart man believeth unto righteousness; and with the mouth confession is made unto salvation (Rom. 10:4–10).

The above passage of Scripture begins with a very important verse. The nature of its interpretation can only be seen by a discussion of the English word *end* before we turn to see the meaning of the original Greek word in the New Testament. What do we mean by the word *end*?

There is no difficulty when we take the word in its common uses. We know what we mean by the end of a field or the end of the rope. If we have enough loose ends of strings or ends of candles, we have a boxful of odds and ends. These usages of the word have to do with space and material. The end of the day and the end of the year are time limitations. The word is also used for death as when a man comes to an untimely end, thus describing his final condition.

In addition to these meanings of the word which refer to space, material, time, and conditions, there is a very important meaning of the word which refers to an aim, a purpose, or the intended result of an action. With all this before us, we return to our text which states that Christ is the end of the law for righteousness to every one that believeth.

The meaning of the word *telos*, the end, depends always on the context. The end of life is its termination. The end of troubles is their transformation. The end of a promise is its fulfillment. The end of our faith is the salvation of our souls (1 Peter 1:9). What is the end of the law? Our text says, "Christ is the end of the law for righteousness to every one that believeth."

New Principles and Methods

The sinner who lived under the law of Moses had strivings that could not be fulfilled. The man who knows the Lord Jesus Christ as his Savior finds that he can enter into the rest and peace, which was provided by Christ. The central section of the epistle to the Hebrews sets forth these truths in such a way that it might be thought that the writer to the Hebrews had taken our text as a point of departure. Listen to these words: "Quite plainly then, there is a definite cancellation of the previous commandment because of its ineffectiveness and uselessness." "For the law made nothing perfect"—it was incapable of bringing anyone to real maturity—"but the bringing in of a better hope did" (Heb. 7:19). It is Christ, this better hope, who is the end of the law, the end of its methods, the end of its priesthood, and the end of its purpose. He is made unto us righteousness and He brings us to this better hope.

It is evident, therefore, that with the coming of Christ there was a complete change of administration that introduced new principles and methods. The change from Old Testament times and methods to those which are in force today was a far greater change than that which was accomplished in the field of government when our land stopped being a colony of England and became a free republic responsible to the people.

Every Jew was familiar with the priesthood of Aaron which governed the religious life of Israel. One of the priests of the Tribe of Levi offered the morning and evening sacrifice every day of the year. The priests were headed by a man who bore the title of High Priest. The Old Testament contains whole books that have to do with the foundation of this priesthood and the maintenance of its work. Exodus, Leviticus, Numbers, and Deuteronomy are filled with details concerning the consecration and service of these earthly priests. Suddenly, the New Testament announces that this priesthood is to be abolished. At the moment Christ died, the great curtain in the temple which separated the holy place from the holiest of all was torn in two, from top to bottom, and God announced that He was through with priesthood and liturgical service.

The Righteousness of Faith

Israel had operated under the law of Moses throughout the fifteen centuries between the giving of the law and the coming of Christ. This was by the order and plan of God. When we come to the New Testament, we discover that the Old Testament was an object lesson or a temporary picture of that which was to be permanent. The Old Testament was the shadow of something that was to be substance. The New Testament might be summarized in its relationship to the Old Testament by saying: Instead of the temple, it is to be Christ; instead of Moses, Christ; instead of Aaron, Christ; instead of the law, Christ; instead of ceremonies, Christ; instead of worship localized in a building, there is to be the eternal, omnipresent Christ.

Law and Grace

The opening verse of our passage is a trumpet shout of triumph that a revolution has taken place and that an entirely new manner of life has been set before men by God. I go back to the illustration of human law and government. The colonists in America felt themselves aggrieved under the colonial administration from England. A great revolution took place. There was war. George Washington led the movement to destroy colonial power and establish an entirely new government that was based on a new constitution. We might say that Washington was the end of English law for government to everyone abiding in the colonies. So we may understand that Christ was the end of the Mosaic law and all its bondage in order to bring in the New Testament as an entirely different constitution from which true liberties could flow in the lives of those who believe. The righteousness of God, which He wished to make effective in the lives of men, is made available under the new conditions of the risen Christ coming to live His life in the hearts of those whom He has redeemed, and in whom He is working out His purposes.

I am no more under the law of Moses as a Christian than I am under the government of England as an American citizen. There has been a revolution; Christ has died. He is risen again, and He lives. It can readily be seen that the fact that I am delivered from the government of England does not mean that I am no longer governed but rather that I am governed by a new constitution. The fact that I am delivered from the law of Moses does not mean that I am lawless but that I have an allegiance to the Lord Jesus Christ who is the very righteousness of God.

Our text now leads to a great contrast between the manner of life which we know as we live under grace and the manner of life which the poor bondmen of the law knew as they lived under its provisions.

After showing that the nature of the law was to establish a code whose righteousness was such that the man under the law had to live completely by the law, an impossible task; the writer now contrasts that desperate condition with the joy of a man who has been freed from the law and is living under grace. This contrast is presented by means of a quotation from the book of Deuteronomy. "For this commandment which I command thee this day, it is not hidden from thee, neither is it far off. It is not in heaven, that thou shouldst say, Who shall go up for us to heaven, and bring it unto us, that we may hear it, and do it? Neither is it beyond the sea, that thou shouldst say, Who shall go over the sea for us, and bring it unto us, that we may hear it, and do it? But the word is very nigh unto thee, in thy mouth, and in thy heart, that thou mayest do it" (30:11–14). The introductory sentence is a positive clause and is followed by a negative clause which states the question. It might be paraphrased: the righteousness which is of faith does not have to say what the man seeking righteousness by law is forced to say.

Paul takes this quotation from a portion of Moses' farewell address and applies it to the situation where the law came to its end even as Moses had come to the end of his life. At the end of the life of Moses, it was not necessary for the people to be in a state of nervous apprehension because their visible leader was removed from them. The word of grace was near to them and they could trust it. Now the argument is that, since the Lord Jesus Christ has come and has died on the cross to fulfill the righteous demands of the law by shedding His blood for the remission of sins, there is therefore no more need of apprehension. The righteousness based on faith does not have fear. There is no fear in grace.

Outward Signs

Furthermore, the very nature of the grace which God has given to us removes us from any form of religion that needs any outward sign or manifestation as a confirmation of the Word of God. Moses made it plain to the children of Israel who stood before Pisgah that they had the law in simple words and that they needed no further manifestation. The signs had all been displayed on Mount Sinai. From thence onward, there was nothing to do but submit to the unequivocal Word which they possessed in their mouths and in their hearts. Israel did not obey the command of Moses for, instead of turning to the Word which was near to them, they began looking for signs. By the time of Christ, they approached the Lord with a request, "Master, we wish to see a sign from you" (Matt. 12:38). The Lord Jesus Christ knew their hearts so well that He was forced to answer, "An evil and adulterous generation seeks for a sign; but no sign shall be given to it except the sign of the prophet Jonah." This seems to have been a stock question. We find it again four chapters further on and Jesus seems to have devised a stock answer to it, for He gives it to them again, word for word (Matt. 16:1–4).

Mark's record of one of these incidents sets forth that "Jesus sighed deeply in His spirit, and said, 'Why does this generation seek a sign?'" (Mark 8:12). Luke records the same question and answer in a completely different framework (Luke 11:16–20), while John brings his account of the request for a sign inside the temple and shows Jesus' answer that they would destroy the temple (of His body) and that He would raise it in three days (John 2:18, 19).

True Worship

One of the main purposes of the Christian faith is to take our minds and hearts away from the things of time and to lift them to the things of eternity and the things of the spirit. Christ announced this when He was here on earth. "The hour is coming, and now is, when the true worshippers will worship the Father in spirit and in truth, for such the Father seeks to worship him. God is spirit, and those who worship him must worship him in spirit and in truth" (John 4:23, 24).

This is the whole way of life for those who know the righteousness of faith. That righteousness does not say, "Who shall ascend into heaven to bring Christ down?" Everything that is necessary for the salvation of the individual has been done by the first coming of the Lord Jesus Christ. Redemption has been fully accomplished, completing God's purposes for this present age. There is nothing that we need for our present pilgrim walk that has not been provided by Christ and made available for us.

The seventh verse of Romans 10 shows that it is not necessary to say, "Who shall descend into the abyss, that is, to bring Christ up from the dead." When Moses originally used this language, he was reminding Israel that they did not have to go across the sea to find some leader. He was talking about the Red Sea and reminding them of their withdrawal from Egypt. When Paul uses the same language, he is not giving an exact quotation, but is paraphrasing the words in order to demonstrate the truth of Christ's nearness to us. Where Moses had spoken of going across the sea, Paul speaks of going down into the abyss into the depths of death. Biblical language always placed the abode of the spirits of the dead *before the time of Christ* within the earth. To the Ephesians, Paul writes, "When Christ ascended on high, he led a host of captives, and he gave gifts unto men. In saying, 'He is ascended,' what does it mean but that he had also descended into the lower parts of the earth? He who descended is he who also ascended far above all the heavens that he might fill all things" (Eph. 4:8–10).

CHAPTER VIII

Now the argument concludes by stating that the Lord Jesus Christ has done everything in the past that needs to be done for individual salvation and that He has done this by dying on the cross. We must not think of His death in terms of the death of any other man. Poets have cried out to the shades of great men of the past and wondered if Caesar, if Charles of Spain or some other could not come back again and lead their disorganized followers. We do not have to go to the abyss of death to seek Christ. The angel told Mary on the day of the resurrection, "He is not here; He is risen, even as he said" (Matt. 28:6).

Thus it is that the living Word is nigh us, even in our hearts. All that we need and all that we want is to be found in the crucified and risen Savior. He lives, and He lives in order to lead and guide us, and to provide for us in every way.

Jesus is Lord

In chapter ten, verse eight, God tells man that He has put the Word of the Gospel very near to the lost creature, even in his mouth and in his heart. He then continues to expand the idea in order to show what the Word of faith is. If the individual shall confess with his mouth that Jesus is Lord and shall believe in his heart that God raised Him from the dead, he shall be saved. The reason for this is then given. With the heart man believes unto righteousness and with the mouth confession is made unto salvation.

There are some problems and some great teaching involved here. First of all, we must agree with practically all commentators that this passage is primarily addressed to the Jews, Paul's brethren according to the flesh. We can come to a deep understanding of the passage if we consider it, first, as a word that is addressed to Israel. We can then expand it to universal proportions and look upon it as a word that describes the transforming work of God in any individual, Jew or Gentile.

The first thing that was necessary for a member of the ancient covenant nation to do was to confess that Jesus Christ was Lord. The Greek here is literally, "if thou shalt confess with thy mouth Jesus, Lord." This is a grammatical construction which must be translated fully, "if thou shalt confess with thy mouth Jesus as thy Lord." It is taken for granted that the hearer has heard the full Gospel. He has been told that certain historical events have happened and that these events are the basis of faith and of salvation. Jesus was a man walking among men. In physical appearance He looked no different from other men and the Scripture plainly says that He was not an outstanding personality. "He has no form nor comeliness, nor any beauty that we should desire him" (Isa. 53:2). Christ did not look like those saccharine pictures which we see of Him as the sallow, bearded man. He lived among men, despised and rejected. He was the average man. He was put on the cross and died an ignominious death. Then God raised Him from the dead. The facts of this life and death and resurrection had been made known to individuals. Did the individual hearer accept these facts? Was this meek and lowly Jesus none other than the Lord Jehovah of Hosts? Was this God's Messiah come to do His eternal work? These were the questions that the individual had to face. There was something more. Not only had these facts to be accepted as historically true, but the individual had to make a personal commitment of his own being to this Messiah; he had to confess that the Jesus is his Lord.

Confessing Christ

It was not possible that there could have been secret belief among his peole. When Jesus was here upon the earth, we read in John's Gospel, "Nevertheless, among the chief rulers also many believed on him; but because of the Pharisees they did not confess him, lest they should be put out of the synagogue: for they loved the praise of men more than the praise of God" (John. 12:42, 43).

There have been those who have wondered why Paul here puts confession before the faith of the heart since in all the epistle up to this point the emphasis has been so strongly upon faith. If the whole passage is looked at, however, it will be seen that there are four phrases, beginning with confession with mouth and going on to belief in the heart, then repeating the matter of belief in the heart and ending, once more, with confession by the mouth. Thus Paul goes from the outward act and manifestation to that which is the real cause of the confession, explains the deep principle of inward faith, and ends with the fact that it must manifest itself in outward life. He is showing that here is a work that must proceed from faith, and that this faith surely produces that work.

The world understands a confession of Christ. When anyone has publicly confessed Christ, the world is astonished if the life is not changed. This is one reason why the unregenerate world publicizes the sins of those who have acknowledged Christ. You would never see a newspaper headline shouting, "Bartender defrauds widow!" Nor would you see a headline that would indicate that it was extraordinary if some fraud had been committed by a doctor, lawyer, prize fighter, merchant or a man of some other profession. Let a man who has been set apart for the ministry of Christ be caught in some sin; then it is good for banner headlines. "Preacher robs couple." That, from the point of view of the newspaper, is a newsworthy item.

CHAPTER VIII

When a dog bites a man, it is not news; but if a man bites a dog, it is news. When an ordinary worldling steals, it is not news; but if a minister of Christ steals, it is national news. Incidentally, such a news item appears so rarely that when it does appear, it is a testimony to the honest lives of the hundreds of thousands of men who have not transgressed. Their confession of Christ has effectively worked in their lives in a practical way. When a man has confessed Christ and transgressed into open sin, the world is so quick to see it that it blazes it in headlines.

The nature of the passage that is before us and that which shall follow through the remainder of the epistle forbids our being fully satisfied with any mechanistic idea of election which makes man no more than an automaton. There are too many scores of passages which speak of man's responsibility and the necessity of man's choice. Here we are confronted with statements that man must confess with his mouth and believe in his heart. There is really only one concerted action here. "Out of the abundance of the heart the mouth speaketh" (Matt. 12:34). We know, of course, that the physical heart is nothing more than a hollow muscular organ which by its dilation and contraction keeps up the circulation of the blood throughout the body. In the course of time, men came to consider the heart as the center of vital functions and the seat of life. From this meaning, in our civilization at least, the word began to be used to describe the mind, including the functions of feeling, volition, and intellect. Thus men came to speak of the eyes of the heart, the ears of the heart, and even of the heart of the heart. The word was reduced in scope to mean the emotional nature as distinguished from the intellectual nature. The intellectual nature was placed in the head, and thus we speak naturally of head and heart as meaning the intellectual and emotional natures together. From this meaning, the word "heart" passed on to signify nothing more than affection, love, or devotion. It is in this sense that we hear it most often in the popular songs of our day. In the Bible we must understand this word to mean the seat of one's inmost thoughts and secret feelings, one's inmost being, the depths of the soul, or to be used as a synonym for the soul.

The early part of the Roman epistle lays great stress on God's part of our redemption; we are justified by the work of the Lord Jesus Christ. The purpose of this work was not merely to give certain people a pleasant exemption from eternal punishment but to show that God is love and that He really loves us and wants us to have the best. The best for man can come only through his being yielded back to God to walk in His way.

An individual must come to the place of total commitment of himself to Jesus Christ as his Lord and Savior, because without this, there is no reality of salvation. The emphasis in our text is on man's part in salvation and we must consider man's responsibility.

Salvation

The confession that the mouth makes unto salvation is not a little speech of acknowledgment of Christ as Savior. It is not the reciting of a creed, even though most orthodox. It is the recognition that Jesus is Lord of the life and the moment by moment confirmation of the life to the image of God's Son. It is the fulfillment in the life of the prayer that our Lord taught His disciples, "Hallowed be Thy Name." What does it mean to be saved? There have been so many well-intentioned and zealous Christians who have gone around asking others whether they are saved that a great many people are familiar with the phrase without knowing the inner meaning of the truth. In fact, many of those who go around asking the question do not always understand what they are asking.

The *Oxford English Dictionary* devotes only a brief paragraph to the word "saved" and, in addition to the meaning that has to do with the saving or economizing of money, it gives but one brief phrase of definition: "delivered from damnation." The Biblical idea is far more than this.

The Greek word *soteria* which has been translated for us as "salvation" was a word known both to the Jews and the pagans. The early Christians, who were nearly all Jews, knew the word as it was used in the Septuagint translation of the Old Testament Scriptures. The pagans knew the word as it was used in their mystery religions. Paul used it because it was the word which was already in the Scriptures and which the Holy Spirit was giving to him to express all that God wants us to know of His divine plans for us; His hopes, His desires, and His longings for us on whom He has so richly set His love: To the pagans, salvation was safety, health and prosperity; but even in pagan usage there was an undertone that carried a meaning that was beyond the present. It was not merely present safety, present health, and present prosperity but also a desire for safety, health, and prosperity that went beyond the grave.

First of all, God's Word teaches that our salvation was something that was accomplished by Christ and which became available to the whole of the human race. We find this thought in such verses as that in which Christ made His pronouncements to the woman at the well: "Woman, you worship you know not what; we know what we worship, for salvation is of the Jews" (John 4:22). This was His declaration that all that He was and all that He was going to accomplish would be in accordance with the prophecies made in the Old Testament. That this salvation would be available to all was set forth in verses such as Peter's statement to the Sanhedrin: "And there is salvation in no one else, for there is no other name under heaven given among men by which we must be saved" (Acts 4:12).

This was the preaching of Paul and Barnabas as they announced that they woud go beyond the limits of their own nation and take the Gospel to all the world. We read in the account of that fateful day in Antioch, "The next Sabbath almost the whole city gathered together to hear the word of God. But when the Jews saw the multitudes, they were filled with jealousy and contradicted what was spoken by Paul and reviled him. Paul and Barnabas spoke out boldly saying, 'It was necessary that the Word of God should be spoken first to you. Since you thrust it from you and judge yourselves unworthy of eternal life, behold, we turn to the Gentiles. For so the Lord has commanded us, saying, I have set you to be a light to the Gentiles, that you may bring salvation to the uttermost parts of the earth'" (Acts 13:44–47). It will be in this sense that Paul will say in the eleventh chapter of Romans, "I ask, have they stumbled so as to fall? By no means! But through their trespass salvation has come to the Gentiles, so as to make Israel jealous" (Rom. 11:11).

Christ has come from heaven and has brought us this perfect salvation by dying for us on the cross. This we can proclaim, this we must proclaim. "Working together with him, then, we entreat you not to accept the grace of God in vain. For he says, 'At the acceptable time I have listened to you and helped you on the day of salvation.' Behold now is the acceptable time; behold now is the day of salvation" (2 Cor. 6:1, 2).

Arising above this definition, we who are believers are able to know much more of salvation than that which is set forth as being potential in Christ. We are able, by faith, to lay hold on that which has been accomplished for us and to know that salvation is our present possession. It was of this that Zechariah prophesied at the time of the birth of the forerunner, John the Baptist. "You, child,.... will go before the Lord to prepare his way, to give knowledge of salvation to his people in the forgiveness of their sins" (Luke 1:77).

In a world of unrest, confusion and frustration, it is possible for us to have this knowledge of salvation that brings in its train all the effectiveness of the peace that passes all understanding (Phil. 4:7). This is a knowledge of salvation which can be our possession without even the slightest doubt. This is the force of the double use of the word *know* in John's blessed statement, "And we know that the Son of God has come and has given us understanding to know him who is true, and we are in him who is true, in his Son Jesus Christ. This is the true God and eternal life" (1 John 5:20).

Furthermore, it was the possession of this salvation and the certain knowledge of it, which was a great factor in the driving power that sent Paul up and down the world as a victim of persecution and in peril from the storms of the elements and the greater storms of the passions of evil men in order that others might possess this same salvation. He wrote to Timothy, "Remember Jesus Christ, risen from the dead, descended from David, as preached in my gospel, the gospel for which I am suffering and bearing fetters, like a criminal. But the word of God is not fettered, therefore I endure everything for the sake of the elect that they may also obtain the salvation which in Christ Jesus goes with eternal glory" (2 Tim. 2:8–10). This ties in with the fact that the righteousness which comes to the heart through Christ will manifest itself in outward confession.

IX

Salvation for All

For the scripture saith, Whosoever believeth on him shall not be ashamed. For there is no difference between the Jew and the Greek: for the same Lord over all is rich unto all that call upon him. For whosoever shall call upon the name of the Lord shall be saved (Rom. 10:11–13).

For the Scripture says, "Whosoever believeth on him shall not be put to shame" (Rom. 10:11). The idea of shame in human literature is a twofold one. There is an evil meaning which has come from the pride of man and a divine meaning which has come from the revelation of God.

The first of these is expressed in an old proverb, "Be not ashamed of anything but to be ashamed." That idea goes back to Aristotle who said, "Shame is the mark of a base man and belongs to a character capable of shameful acts." Pride is the father of such shame as God says, "When pride comes, then comes shame" (Prov. 11:2), and such shame soon disintegrates into a shame of poverty or thrift or of some other quality. This in turn causes men, because they do not wish to be thought poor, to live beyond their means, the great sin which the Bible calls "emulation" (Gal. 5:20), lumping it with impurity and idolatry. All such shame is shameful.

Proper Shame

Proper shame, however, is a part of repentance. When there is no shame for sin, there can be neither acknowledgment of the sin nor repentance. When Adam fled from God in the garden of Eden, he was forced to acknowledge the reason—he was afraid. We are told that there was no shame in the state of innocence. (Gen. 2:25). With the loss of innocence there came a shame that brought fear.

It was only then that God spoke to them and made the promise of grace which would make salvation possible for them and all the human race.

Those who will not bow before God will be brought to the place where they will be bowed in spite of themselves. In that day, the nakedness of men's hearts will be made manifest. Those who have had their sins blotted out by the atonement provided through the death of Jesus Christ will be able to stand boldly before God in that day, while those who have refused to acknowledge their need of Him and to confess Him as their Savior will be brought to open shame and confusion. Let us look at some of the Bible teachings on this subject.

If we turn to the concordance and go down the list of verses which speak of shame or of being ashamed, it will soon be noted that there are scores of verses in which God states that He will put to shame those who have not acknowledged Him. It will be well to quote some of these verses. "They shall be turned back and utterly put to shame, who trust in graven images, who say to molten images, You are our gods" (Isa. 42:17). "All who make idols are nothing, and the things they delight in do not profit; their witnesses neither see nor know, that they may be put to shame. Who fashions a god or casts an image that is profitable for nothing? Behold, all his fellows shall be put to shame, and the craftsmen are but men; let them all assemble, let them stand forth; they shall be terrified, they shall be put to shame together" (Isa. 44:9–11). "Wherefore thus says the Lord God: behold, my servants shall eat but you shall be hungry; behold my servants shall drink but you shall be thirsty; behold my servants shall rejoice but you shall be put to shame" (Isa. 65:13).

There is one of these verses which has to be paraphrased in order to be understood. There are those who hate God's people and even come to the point where they sneer at those who put their trust in Him. They scoff at our belief that Christ will come again bringing victory and joy to His people. They say, "Well, well! so you believe that Christ is coming and that you are going to come out on top? Well, let Him come and be glorified and we will look at our triumphing. Ha! Ha!" It may seem extraordinary that there should be people who would think and talk in this way, but we must not forget that the Adamic heart is a heart of unbelief and that men fundamentally hate the true God of redemption and want to be God for themselves. The verse which we have paraphrased reads as follows: "Hear the word of the Lord, you who tremble at His word. Your brethren who hate you and cast you out for My name's sake have said, Let the Lord be glorified, that we may see your joy, but it is they who shall be put to shame" (Isa. 66:5).

The shame into which some shall be brought and from which others shall escape is not merely the eternal shame of being separated from God or the opposite joy of being joined to Him forever. There is here the revelation of the judgment in which men shall be brought to acknowledge what they are in themselves and to stand divested of all the pretense in which they have clothed themselves. The world lives

CHAPTER IX

in an artificial state of self-deception, but the judgment will come and remove all this. God has described it, "Behold, I am laying in Zion for a foundation stone a tested stone, a precious cornerstone, of a sure foundation; He who believes will not be in haste. And I will make justice the line and righteousness the plummet; and hail will sweep away the refuge of lies, and waters will overflow the shelters" (Isa. 28:16, 17).

Judgment Coming

Because of the fact that we are unable to see into the recesses of men's hearts and do not know the motives which animate them in their choices, we are told that we are to form no judgments until the time of the end. It is the knowledge that we are to appear before the judgment seat of Christ that causes us to be very severe with ourselves and to adopt an attitude of compassion and tenderness toward all other men. Though we may condemn evil actions, we will love even evil men and desire their salvation.

So it was that Paul wrote, "This is how one should regard us, as servants of Christ and stewards of the mysteries of God. Moreover it is required of stewards that they be found trustworthy. But with me it is a very small thing that I should be judged by you or by any human court. I do not even judge myself. I am not aware of anything against myself, but I am not thereby acquitted. It is the Lord who judges me. Therefore do not pronounce judgment before the time, before the Lord comes, who will bring to light the things now hidden in darkness and will disclose the purpose of the heart" (1 Cor. 4:1–5).

God has told us throughout His Word, and He is telling us in our text that the day will come when men, all men, shall be brought into judgment. The time of judgment may differ for those who have trusted in Christ and for those who have not; we believe that the bane does differ and that the two groups will appear at different judgments. The fact remains that there will be judgment and those who have not trusted in Christ will stand shamed, condemned and judged; while those who have taken their stand with Christ shall not be ashamed. Issues of eternity are settled here and now and those who refuse to bow to Him now in grateful praise will, before they are separated from God into outer darkness forever, be forced to bow before Him.

Salvation for All

Before dealing with the next passage of our text, it is necessary to establish the translation. In the Authorized Version we read: "For there is no difference between the Jew and the Greek; for the same Lord over all is rich unto all that call upon him." The various versions give different renderings of the original Greek. A composite translation would read as follows: "For there is no distinction between Jew and Greek, [that is, between Jew and non-Jew], for the same Lord is Lord over all, generous, bestowing His riches on all who call upon Him."

All men are alike in God's sight. The free offer of salvation that is made to all men is grounded and founded on the fact that God has made Jesus Christ Lord of all, that He gave richly and generously to all who come to Him because He has opened a fountain of all blessing in Christ, and that He can make known the riches of His grace through Him.

First it should be noted that all the promises that are set forth are based on quotations from the Old Testament. The apostle was addressing himself primarily to the Jews, but secondarily to all men. He wanted all to know that God had been consistent throughout all the centuries, and that salvation, both before and since the time of Christ, had been set forth as simple faith in God's Messiah, the Lord Jesus Christ.

We must further note that our text teaches that God has made Christ to be Lord over all. There will be no help for the man who has underestimated God's opinion about the Lord Jesus Christ. In the sight of the Father, Christ is everything. God will have no thought for anything or anybody that has not moved toward conformity with the Lord Jesus. "What think ye of Christ?" (Matt. 22:42). This is the most important question that any man can ever face. Our answer will determine our eternal state and our eternal position in that state. Christ "is the image of the invisible God," He tells us, "the first-born of all creation; for in him all things were created, in heaven and on earth, visible and invisible, whether thrones or dominions or principalities or authorities—all things were created through him and for him. He is before all things and in him all things hold together" (Col. 1:15–17). Thus the Holy Spirit writes to the believers in the town of Colossae. To the church at Philippi, He revealed all that the Lord Jesus had done in leaving the throne of God in heaven in order to go down to the earth as a man and submit Himself to death, even to death by crucifixion. It was because of this, He said, that "God has highly exalted him and bestowed on him the name that is above every name, that at the name of Jesus every knee should bow, in heaven and on earth and under the earth, and every tongue confess that Jesus Christ is Lord, to the glory of God the Father" (Phil. 2:9–11).

Our text also indicates that the Lord Jesus, who is Lord of all, makes freely available all of His riches to anyone who will come and avail himself of them. It is one thing to possess great wealth and another thing to make it available to those who have not been so fortunate in life. Miserliness is an abominable thing while generosity is a divine attribute. Generosity is the outflow of love and God is love.

We come now to one of the great texts of Scriptures. "For whosoever calls on the name of the Lord shall be saved." It is a part of the great simplicity of the Gospel which sets before man the open way to God and lets him know how easily God can be reached and how accessible He is to all men at all times. Surely God has made the way of salvation so simple that no man can claim any excuse whatsoever.

Our text is one of the great universals of the Bible and reaches to the heart of every man. Whether or not you will answer when God speaks to you is another question. The way of salvation is clear and open. Your response is deep in the recesses of your heart. The very proclamation of truth adds to the responsibility of everyone that hears. A man may be unwilling to listen to truth and may stifle the voice of God as easily as a man can reach out his hand and tune out a radio program. But man is fully accountable and will give answer to God for what he has done with the good news that is proclaimed to him.

The good news is that you may be saved—that eternal life may enter into you and that you may enter into eternal life. The good news is that God has nothing against you and that He has done all that is necessary to have you reconciled to Himself.

There are four parts to our text but I am going to place the main emphasis on one of the parts. I will not tarry long here on the nature of salvation because we have treated that at some length in previous studies. It is not necessary that we should reiterate the universality of the call; "whosoever" means you, me or anybody else. There is no member of the human race who may not be included in this "whosoever."

The Name of the Lord

We will expand slightly on the third point, the name of the Lord, and then go on to find the meaning of what God wants us to do in calling upon Him. "The name of the Lord," we read in Proverbs, "is a strong tower; the justified man runs into it and is safe" (Prov. 18:10). The previous verse in our Roman's study sets forth that the name of our Savior is the Lord who is Lord of all. This is the declaration of His identity. We are not dealing with "the meek and lowly Jesus," but we are dealing with the One who has been appointed by God to judge the world at His return to the earth (Heb. 1:2, Acts 17:31). The wonder of the name of the Lord is that it began in the incarnation with the announcement from the angels that the baby would be born without a human father, that He would be begotten by the Holy Spirit, and that His name would be called Jesus, Savior, because He would save His people from their sins. Everything that God has for man is included in the name of the Lord Jesus Christ. Everything that man needs in any realm is to be found in the name of the Lord Jesus Christ. This is the great comprehensive that includes all things, material and spiritual. This is that which enfolds the emotions, satisfies the intelligence, quiets the conscience, and brings peace to the heart. This is that which tames the willful, balances the neurotic, straightens out the confused, and gives direction to the man who has been going around in circles. When all other streams have dried, this is the full flowing fountain. When all other things are shaken, this is that which remains. When physical death comes, this is that which causes the soul and spirit to issue forth into life eternal.

Calling on His Name

God announces that whosoever calls on this name shall be saved. What does calling on the name of the Lord mean? A man may open his mouth in a time of distress and cry, "Lord, help me!" without necessarily calling on the name of the Lord in the sense of our text. We might say that he has the words but not the music. Calling on the name of the Lord is going out of the whole of being, heart, soul, mind and strength, in a movement that has turned away from any hope in self and that has come to an utter confiding in the Lord Jesus Christ.

If we page through the Word of God, we find scores of instances of men calling on the name of the Lord. Three times in the life of Abraham we find him calling on the name of the Lord. It is significant that each time when he calls on the name of the Lord Jehovah, he is standing at an altar of blood sacrifice. This shows us that, from the beginning, calling on the Lord was connected with the blood atonement. In the story of Elijah, we have the great incident of his conflict with the priests of Baal. A sacrifice was to be prepared by each camp. Then, said Elijah to these false priests, "Let two bulls be given to us; and let them choose one bull for themselves, and cut it in pieces and lay it on the wood, and put no fire to it; and I will prepare the other bull and lay it on the wood, and put no fire to it. And you call on the name of your god and I will call on the name of the Lord; and the God who answers by fire he is God" (1 Kings 18:23, 24). Here the calling on the name of the Lord was not only connected with the blood sacrifice but it was something that put God to the test and showed the utter faith which Elijah had in Him.

In the Psalms God tells His people to call upon Him and tells them what He does for them when they obey Him. We read in the fiftieth Psalm, "Call upon me in the day of trouble; I will deliver you and you shall glorify me" (v. 15). In a later Psalm, God has Asaph sing, "In distress you called and I delivered you, I answered you in the secret place of thunder" (Ps. 81:7). There are many other verses which speak of the blessing of calling on the name of the Lord and the misery that comes from not calling on Him, but I will confine myself to two that are found in the prophecy of Jeremiah.

CHAPTER IX

The first of the texts is of double importance because it enlarges still further on this idea of calling on the Lord, noting some of the conditions attached to the calling.

God is speaking to His ancient people and telling them of the deliverance that He has in His purpose for them. We read, "For I know the plans I have for you, says the Lord, plans for welfare and not for evil, to give you a future and a hope. Then you will call upon me and come and pray to me and I will hear you. You will seek me and find me; when you seek me with all your heart, I will be found by you, says the Lord" (Jer. 29:11–14). This helps us to see that calling upon the Lord is to seek Him with our whole heart, that we may come to Him, that we may pray to Him.

The other passage in Jeremiah is a declaration of the power of God and an invitation for us to avail ourselves of that power by calling upon Him. We read, "Behold I am the Lord, the God of all flesh; is anything too hard for me? . . . Call to me and I will answer you and will tell you great and hidden things which you have not known" (Jer. 32:27; 33:3).

Putting all of these thoughts together, we may arrive at the conclusions that to call upon the name of the Lord is to believe all that the name of the Lord stands for; to know the Lord in His qualities as Savior God, Lord of all; to approach Him through the altar of the cross; to recognize that there is no strength in ourselves but that all power dwells in Him; and to commit ourselves to Him in faith, desiring that He should act for us as He sees our need.

We know both from the study of the Word and from our own lives that calling on the name of the Lord can be either a short experience or a long one. At times when we are in danger and trouble, our calling on the Lord is like the stabbing upthrust of a drowning man who clutches at that which can take him out of trouble. At other times when we are in sorrow and tribulation, our calling on the Lord is like the continual leaning of a wounded man who comes to rest upon a bed. Our calling on the Lord may well be the sudden thrust that turns into a constant trust.

X

The Word for the World

How then shall they call on him in whom they have not believed? and how shall they believe in him of whom they have not heard? and how shall they hear without a preacher? And how shall they preach, except they be sent? as it is written, How beautiful are the feet of them that preach the gospel of peace, and bring glad tidings of good things! But they have not all obeyed the gospel. For Isaiah saith, Lord, who hath believed our report? So then faith cometh by hearing, and hearing by the word of God (Rom. 10:14–17).

The Gospel has been brought to the earth by God the Father through the Lord Jesus Christ. The good news has been proclaimed. God does not have anything against any man who will come and be submitted to Him through Christ, but there are masses of people who are unaware of the good news and what it is. The problem is to get the remedy to those who need it.

From time to time we read human interest stories in the newspapers of expeditions that take needed remedies to centers of epidemic. A plane will fly penicillin to a marooned village in the arctic; an iron lung will be flown to a remote place where an almost breathless patient awaits it; the Red Cross will press its way into a flooded area to inoculate those who are in danger of typhoid. All of these stories pale into insignificance when compared to the need of getting the Gospel to people who are lost without it, whose danger is not a momentary epidemic or physical death but an eternal separation from God.

The Good News has been proclaimed, but men must know about it if they are going to turn away from lesser and ineffective remedies to the one thing that can bring life and peace. The good news is that God loves us and has come in Christ to die for us and to bear the curse for sin. The wrath of God is stilled forever; Christ is now able to take even the vilest sinner into God's holy presence without fouling Heaven. How is the sinner going to call upon God for salvation if he does not believe in God and His Son?

True Belief

The whole process of blessing is set forth before us as a chain of several links. The sinner stands there in all his need. He must call on God. Before he can call on God, he must believe in Him. He must also believe Him. To believe in Him is to believe that He is and that He answers when men call upon Him. We have it set forth in the epistle to the Hebrews. "Without faith it is impossible to please him. For whoever would draw near to God must believe that he exists and that he rewards those who seek him" (11:6). In addition to believing that He exists, the individual must believe God when He speaks. It is possible to believe in God without believing God. God has spoken and His declaration is set forth in the Bible. If one believes that God exists without believing what He has spoken, he has not the reality of faith.

It is possible for men to believe that God exists, to believe that He has spoken, and to stop short of applying the truth to their own personal need. It is even possible for men to be so occupied with the mechanics of the Bible itself that they fail to see the reason why God gave the Scriptures. This was the great error of the Pharisees in the days of Christ. They were men who had studied the Old Testament Scriptures to the point of fanaticism. Their study of the mechanics of the Scriptures had blinded them to the purpose and meaning of the Scriptures. God had given the Old Testament for the one purpose of foreshadowing the Lord Jesus Christ. This was what Christ said to the men who rose against Him. We read in the fourth Gospel, "you search the Scriptures," (and I believe that there was a note of judgment in His remark), "because you think that in them you have eternal life; and it is they that bear witness to me; yet you refuse to come to me that you may have life" (John 5:39, 40). It is this same error that exists today among many who cling very closely to the Bible. They spend so much time on the Bible itself that they fail to look through the Bible to see the Lord Jesus Christ.

Some time ago we went to Atlantic City to preach in one of the churches there for several days. It was off season and one of the great hotels gave the church, one of its loveliest suites for us to enjoy. We looked out across the Atlantic with its ever-changing moods and enjoyed its beauty to the full. Suppose that a young friend who lived in Iowa and who had never had the privilege of journeying to the coast should have asked us to write him about the ocean. What would you think if we wrote as follows: "We have a beautiful room with a picture window that gives us a sweeping view of the ocean. The window is twelve feet two inches long and four feet eight inches high. It is divided into three sections. We have taken a scraping of the glass and have had it analyzed and can tell you the chemical formula of the glass. We have had an expert from one of the great glass companies tell us all about the glass and we are giving you herewith a history of the invention and development of glass. The glass is set in steel frames that are painted black. We have had the steel and the paint analyzed and you can read the analysis in our second and third studies affixed to this letter. We have discovered that the panes of glass are kept in the frames by a putty composition. We have scraped down some of this putty and are giving you a long addendum on its chemical composition. Finally, we have inquired of the hotel management and found out their method of keeping the windows clean. You will be delighted to know from the subjoined study the whole process of the window-cleaning and the formula of the special detergent needed to cope with the salt spray from the ocean. In closing, let us say that we hope you have enjoyed our study of the ocean."

We smile at such a farcical parable. It must be admitted that there are people who can name for you the books of the Bible, give you the history of the Jewish people, list the kings of Judah and Israel along with a mass of background material about the written Word of God, but who seem to forget that the Bible exists only to bring us to the Lord Jesus Christ. He is the ocean beyond the window. The young man might decide that seeing the ocean was not worth the trip to the Atlantic coast. If it were no more than a study of the window through which the ocean might be seen, he would be right. How many people have been turned away from the road that leads to the Lord Jesus Christ by the inept way in which some, who count themselves among His most zealous followers, point not to the Lord Jesus Christ but to the mechanics by which God has brought Him to us?

Now I will not be misquoted. I am not lessening my concept of the Word of God. I believe that "all Scripture is God-breathed, and that it is profitable" (2 Tim. 3:16) for all the things for which God gave it. But at the same time, however, we must insist that God gave it in order that we should look through it and beyond it to the Lord Jesus Christ. If your concept of the Bible does not bring to your life the warm compassion of the Savior, you have not seen the Word of God aright. If your knowledge of the Bible does not give you an integrity that makes your word as good as your bond, you have not seen the Word of God aright. If you can rise from reading the Word of God and go to a life of petty gossip or inane pastimes, you have not seen the Word of God aright.

Witnessing

"How shall they believe in him of whom they have not heard?" If we look at our text in reverse, we find that if people have not heard the proclamation of the good news in Christ, they cannot believe it; if they have not believed it they are not in a position to call upon the name of the Lord for salvation. We find that salvation comes only from a personal commitment to the facts about Christ, that He died and rose again as the Savior for sinners. Public confession of Jesus Christ as Lord and belief in the heart that God raised Him from the dead are the personal elements that lead to salvation. With the heart man believes unto righteousness and with the mouth confession is made unto salvation. So it would seem that there is no hope for any man who has not been reached by the Gospel.

Returning once more to our text and going forward to the next link in the chain, we find it stated that men cannot hear saving faith without a preacher. There is an important reason why we must analyze this word. The Greek uses the verb *kerusso* which is found sixty-one times in the New Testament. Fifty-three times it is translated as a verb *to preach*; five times it is translated as a verb *to publish*; twice it is translated as a verb *to proclaim*. The sixty-first time, here in our text, the participle form is translated as a noun, *a preacher*. Beyond question the verb should have been rendered as a verb and it is a sad thing to find it as a noun. A. T. Robertson, the great Greek grammarian, rightly translates it, "how shall they hear without one preaching?"* Phillips reads, "how can they hear unless someone proclaims him?"

The call to proclaim the truth has been given to everyone who trusts in Christ. From the divine point of view there is no such division as that which men have made between clergy and laymen. All believers are alike in the sight of God and all are on the same level. It is true that God has declared that some should be set aside as elders to rule in the church but they have no special access to God, and, above all, they do not stand as mediators between men and God.

Paul then makes a powerful plea for missions. "How shall they preach except they be sent?" Note that Paul does not make a plea for "foreign missions" but simply "missions." In the sight of God there is no such thing as "home missions." Every soul is an alien from heaven and those who live in the same house with us and do not know the good news must be brought to hear it as much as the farthest soul on our globe. Conversely, any soul who lives on even the remotest island or in the depths of the remotest jungle has a claim upon us that the good news should be brought to him.

What is it that sends the herald of the Gospel? There are many who go out with some religious message. Are they the voices of men who speak for God? There are several possible sources of a religious message. The devil may send messages to confuse men. Men may band together and send men who do not know the truth and who preach error. Men may decide within themselves that they are going out

---

* A. T. Robertson, *Word Pictures in the New Testament*, used by permission of Broadman Press, Nashville, Tenn.

with a religious message. Finally, there are those who are chosen by God and sent forth by Him. Let us look at these various types of religious speakers.

Religious Messengers

First, the Bible teaches plainly that there are religious messengers who are sent out by the devil. The Lord Jesus Christ flatly told the religious leaders of His day that they were not from the God and Father of the Lord Jesus but that they were sent by Satan. Remember that these words are the words of our Lord Jesus. "'I speak of what I have seen with my Father and you do what you have heard from your father.' They answered Him, 'Abraham is our father.' Jesus said to them, 'If you were Abraham's children, you would do what Abraham did, but now you seek to kill me, a man who has told you the truth which I heard from God; this is not what Abraham did. You do what your father did.' They said to Him, 'We were not born of fornication; we have our father, even God.' Jesus said to them, 'If God were your father, you would love me, for I proceeded and came forth from God; I came not of my own accord but he sent me. Why do you not understand what I say? It is because you cannot bear to hear my word. You are of your father the devil and your will is to do your father's desire. He was a murderer from the beginning and has nothing to do with the truth because there is no truth in him. When he lies, he speaks according to his own nature, for he is a liar and the father of lies.'" (John 8:38–44).

In the second place, there are messengers who are sent out by men without the stamp of God's approval. Of these there may be several types. Some will be sent out by children of the devil as in the first instance. But there are others who are sent out by men who are honest, sincere, and even true believers in Christ. Since it is impossible for men to read the hearts of men, there is always the possibility that unsaved men will be ordained or sent out to the mission field. The more organizational a church group is, the greater the danger that there will be time servers who enter the ministry or go to the mission field without having been sent by God. The more spiritual a group or committee is, the greater probability that they will handle the human side of the work in a spiritual manner and send out men who are truly chosen by God.

In the third place, there are men who go out to give a religious message, that may or may not be the Christian message, entirely on their own psychological responsibility without having been sent by God.

Finally, there are those who are truly sent by God. These latter are marked by the fact that they are faithful to the message of the Gospel, exalting the Lord Jesus Christ, proclaiming to men the good news of salvation through Him, and bidding men to turn from their sins and come to Christ as Savior and Lord. They back all of their proclamations by the authority of the Bible, the Word of God, and they call Christians to lives of holiness while they, themselves are living examples of holiness.

Ordained of God

Unless a man is divinely sent to preach the Word, his ministry will be ineffective to produce faith and life in those to whom he ministers. God must do the sending. I always tell young men who ask me about entering the ministry that they should never become ministers if they can possibly help it. If a man could be satisfied as president of the United States, as president of a bank or a college, as a pitcher for a big-league ball team, or in another position of honor or distinction; he has not been called to the ministry. God has not sent him. When God sends a man, there is a yearning, churning, burning inside him. Like Paul he must cry, "For though I preach the gospel, I have nothing to glory of: for necessity is laid upon me; yea, woe is unto me, if I preach not the gospel" (1 Cor. 9:16). This must be the heart feeling of everyone who has been sent with the Gospel.

True preachers of the Gospel are sent in the same manner that the Lord Jesus Christ was sent from the Father in heaven. He, Himself, declared this truth on the very day of His resurrection. The disciples were in the upper room to which they had fled because they were so afraid of the same persecutors who had put Christ to death. Suddenly the Lord Jesus Christ stood among them in all His resurrection power and glory. He calmed them by saying, "Peace be unto you. And when he had so said, he showed them his hands and his side. Then were the disciples glad when they saw the Lord. Then said Jesus to them again, peace be unto you: as my Father hath sent me, even so send I you" (John 20:19–21).

It should be noted that Christ said twice, "Peace be unto you." The first peace that He gives is the peace of the knowledge of forgiven sin. We know that we have passed from death to life through the work He accomplished in dying for us on the cross. The second time He said, "Peace be unto you," it was in connection with sending forth His disciples. It is impossible to understand our text in Romans without understanding what happened here in this further commissioning of the disciples. Our text says, "How shall they preach except they be sent?" Jesus said, "As my Father hath sent me, even so send I you."

That this divine sending was not confined to the twelve disciples is proved by many further references in the New Testament. Christ certainly did not found an ecclesiastical hierarchy. Christ founded a community of believers among whom there was to be a spiritual equality, in honor preferring one another. We turn to the first chapter of the Book of Acts and read that the last words Jesus spoke while He was here on earth refer to this same subject: "But you shall receive power when the Holy Spirit has come upon you and you shall be my witnesses" (Acts. 1:8). That this went beyond the twelve is shown in the next paragraph (v. 15) by the fact that there were one hundred and twenty who were called disciples. We turn the page and find the number of the disciples given as five thousand (4:4) and we discover that "they were all filled with the Holy Spirit, and spoke the word of God with boldness" (4:31). The next verse adds, "And the multitude of them that believed were of one heart and one soul" (v. 32).

Personal Redemption

What is the message that we preach? "As it is written, How beautiful are the feet of them that preach the gospel of peace and bring glad tidings of good things!" How important then that those who know the truth of God should set forth nothing but that truth. The only diversity that is allowable is that of the man who shows one single diamond but turns the facets so that new and flashing lights may reveal the depth of the stone. When Paul began to declare the truth to the Gentiles, the people who had possessed the covenant truth of God for two thousand years were moved to indignation. There can be no doubt that the Old Testament called upon Israel to be a group of missionaries, taking the truth to all men, but they turned inward upon themselves and became satisfied to see others go past them to their doom.

The Apostle Paul asks, how can the Gentiles ever come to the knowledge of salvation if it is not preached to them? The Jews knew from their own prophets that salvation was confined to those who call upon the name of the Lord. How could other nations call on Him of whom they had not heard? How could they hear without a preacher? This is the same thought that the Holy Spirit expresses to Paul for the bringing of the message of redemption that is bound up with the first coming of the Messiah, the Lord Jesus Christ.

This verse is quoted from the prophecy of Isaiah and the Holy Spirit eliminates one phrase in order to make the application true to the spreading of the Gospel in our day. In Isaiah we read, "How beautiful upon the mountains are the feet of him who brings good tidings, who publishes peace, who brings good tidings of good, who publishes salvation, who says to Zion, Your God reigns" (Isa. 52:7).

Paul leaves out the phrase *upon the mountains* because the message which the Gospel preacher brings is not one of good government and peace on earth among men of ill will. The message that we bring is a message of personal redemption.

CHAPTER X

Christ has died and risen again; He has gone back to the throne of God to pour blessings upon those who will trust in Him, even while they live in the midst of a crooked and perverse generation (Phil. 2:15).

Most definitely we must not look upon this quotation in the New Testament as being the ultimate fulfillment of the prophecy in the Old Testament. It is not a fulfillment; it is an application. The great fulfillment is yet to come. Even now, those who carry the good news of salvation have special honors given to them by God. Their coming is declared to be beautiful.

Faith and the Word

Those who carry the good news of salvation have not only special honors given them by God but the miracle power of the Word of God accompanies their message. "So then faith comes by hearing, and hearing by the word of God." The interrelationship of faith and the hearing of the Word of God is at the heart of the whole process of transforming an individual from a child of wrath into a child of God. It is by the transforming power of the Word, faith laying hold on the Word, that a man ceases to be a child of disobedience and becomes a child of obedient faith.

Our text is often quoted in the King James Version but it needs to be restated in the light of modern knowledge of the Greek text. The Revised Standard Version reads, "So faith comes from what is heard, and what is heard comes by the preaching of Christ." Phillips reads, "Belief, you see, can only come from hearing the message and the message is the word of Christ." The first thing that strikes us in the latter translations is that we are presented with the Word of Christ and not the Word of God. Fundamentally, it is the same thing, but the Greek clearly speaks of the Word of Christ. Grammatically, it is an objective genitive and is translated, *the Word about Christ*. We should also note that there are two different prepositions in the Greek, both of them translated "by" in the King James Version. A very literal rendering would be, "So then faith comes out of what is heard, and what is heard comes through the Word about Christ."

We have already dealt with the fact that this hearing has nothing to do with the ears. We are not concerned here with the physical process of the communication of ideas by sound waves. A blind man can hear through his fingertips as he reads the message in Braille; a deaf man can hear the message through his eyes as he reads the Word of God. This hearing is a process that takes place in the soul. The Word does its work and faith does its work; the two combine to bring life from the dead and light out of darkness.

We are not lowering the place of the written word of God when we accept the true translation of this passage. Faith comes out of hearing and hearing through the

Word about Christ. This is true, but we must understand that the Word about Christ is presented to us in the written Word, the Bible. We have seen that the central theme of the Bible is the Lord Jesus Christ. We believe that it is safe to say that God had no purpose in giving the divine revelation other than the exaltation of the Lord Jesus Christ through the presenation of the message of grace that makes it possible for guilty sinners to be transformed into the likeness of the Eternal Son of God.

It is through the word about the inner meaning of the death of Christ that faith is built into the life of an individual. What God is telling us here is that faith feeds upon the Word about Christ, growing and growing as we have more of that Word. It should go without saying that I am not exalting the printed page above the living Lord Jesus Christ. The word about Christ is not to be taken as a mechanical or detached thing, but as that which leads us into the heart of all that He is and all that He came to do for us. It is not by reading the Bible through and through or by memorizing chapters and verses that one is going to grow in faith. Reading the Bible is important and memorizing Scripture is important, but it is the personal absorption of the truth that is going to cause growth in the life of faith. Faith must be rooted more deeply than merely in mind and memory.

The secret of faith is a simple one—it is feeding upon Jesus Christ. This is of the utmost importance in developing our Christian life and experience. Faith comes from a message that is heard. Faith does not come from a message that is merely listened to. This is what our Lord meant when He said so often, "He that has ears to hear, let him hear."

As we study the written Word, we must never lose the reality of the living Word which is to know Christ Himself. We must keep in mind that it is in the knowledge of the Bible that we are going to find the increase of our faith. It may be true that a man can come to a limited knowledge of the Savior with a limited knowledge of the Bible, but it must be understood that a man can never come to a great knowledge of the Savior without a great knowledge of the written Word of God. Faith comes from getting to know God personally. We can learn the ways of God and can fall into line with His desires and plans by seeing in the Bible how He acted under various circumstances as He dealt with men. As we see Him in action, we come to understand Him and to know Him. As we come to know Him, faith grows with great increase. Faith comes out of what is heard and what is heard comes through the Word about Christ.

XI

God's Disobedient People

But I say, have they not heard? Yes, truly, their sound went into all the earth, and their words unto the ends of the world. But I say, Did not Israel know? First Moses says, I will provoke you to jealousy by those that are no people, and by a foolish nation I will anger you. But Isaiah is very bold, and says, I was found of them that sought me not, I was made manifest to them that asked not after me. But to Israel he says, All day long I have held out my hands to a disobedient and contrary people (Rom. 10:18–21).

There is no possible ground for any argument which will make God narrow, sectarian, or nationalistic. God created the human race and, though mankind has departed from God and brought the curse which accompanies sin, the love of God goes out to all men. His arms are stretched out still to welcome any and all who will repent from their evil ways and come back to Him through His Son Jesus Christ.

A Universal Gospel

It seems strange to us to think that this teaching was once considered new, bold and outrageous, but such is the case. When the Holy Spirit first brought the true Gospel to Paul, it seemed to the men of Israel to be daring, horrible even, to think those who were considered to be dogs of Gentiles should have an opportunity to share in the love of God and to participate in the benefits of His grace. Paul, constantly conflicting with Jewish believers, was forced to contend with the foremost of the twelve disciples and to win them over from their narrow sectarianism. He succeeded with them, but he did not succeed with others.

The second chapter of Galatians clearly reveals that James, Peter and John had no true concepts of the meaning of Christianity. They had gone back to a legalism that is alien to the doctrine of free grace, and only grudgingly at first did they accept the truth as God had given it through Paul. Peter was so mixed up that Paul had to oppose him to his face because he stood condemned as a believer in Christ who had gone back to the ignorance of legalism. We read, "For before certain men came from James, he ate with the Gentiles; but when they came he drew back and separated himself, fearing the circumcision party. And with him the rest of the Jews acted insincerely, so that even Barnabas was carried away by their insincerity. But when I saw that they were not straightforward about the truth of the gospel, I said to Peter before them all, If you, though a Jew, live like a Gentile and not like a Jew, how can you compel the Gentiles to live like Jews?" (Gal. 2:12–14). Paul then continues to set forth the whole doctrine of salvation by grace through faith.

In the light of the fact that the leading apostles of Jesus Christ did not understand the great realities of what had been accomplished by the death and resurrection of their Lord and Savior, it is not astonishing that others of their race, who had not believed in Jesus Christ at all, were unable to understand the direction God was taking in orienting salvation toward the whole of the human race. Jewish tradition was completely in error in thinking that salvation was only for the twelve tribes, the sons of Jacob. They had simply misinterpreted the laws that God had given through Moses four hundred years after Abraham, and had decided that these laws gave them an exclusive right to the true God of the universe and that nobody else could approach Him. It was true that God had chosen the twelve tribes of Israel for a particular purpose, but they should have been intense missionaries, bringing the *goyim*, the heathen, into the tribes and expanding constantly their number to include all who could be induced to approach God through admission to the tribes and then through the sacrifice of the Jewish altar. Enough centuries of their failure to be true missionaries had now passed; God had broken away from the restrictions given by Moses in order to go back to the greater principle that had been promised through Abraham.

No-God and No-People

Moses, before he died, repeated the words of the law to Israel and set forth the truths of the covenant which God had made with Abraham. In a wonderful song he recounted the grace which God had shown for His people and then began to tell of the rebellion of the people toward God. "But Jeshurun waxed fat, and kicked, (you waxed fat; you grew thick; you became sleek) then he forsook God who made him and scoffed at the Rock of his salvation. They stirred him to jealousy with strange gods; with abominable practices they provoked him to anger. They sacrificed to demons which were no gods, to gods they had never known, to new gods that had come in of late, whom your fathers had never dreaded" (Deut. 32:15–17). Then Moses recounts that because of this great sin of the people, God had to turn against them. God speaks, saying, "I will hide my face from them; I will see what their end will be, for they are a perverse generation, children in whom is no faithfulness. They have stirred me to jealousy with what is no god; they have provoked me with their idols. So I will stir them to jealousy with those who are no people; I will provoke them with a foolish nation" (Deut. 32:20, 21).

The contrast between "no-god" and "no-people" is very striking. Anything that any man ever becomes is the result of the blessing of God. God owes no man a blessing, but God gives every man some blessings. In His sovereignty He chose to select one family through which the line of the Messiah should come and in which the Lord Jesus Christ should be born. This was the purpose of His election of the nation of Israel. God selected the Jews in order that there might be the royalty of David, the virginity of Mary, and the birth of the Savior. God selected Palestine in order that there might be a place, a foot square, on which the cross could be erected on which the Son of God might die for the redemption of sinners. That land is still precious in His sight because the Mount of Olives is there, and the feet of the Lord of Glory will stand there at the second coming of Christ. Oh! If only man would learn that God has no purposes in human history apart from the Lord Jesus Christ.

For these special purposes God chose Abraham and the people of Israel. They were to be the heart from which the Savior would come, and they were to be the nucleus into which all mankind was to be brought for the special blessings that God would give. Other peoples had to be outside at first in order to exhibit the nature of God in His hatred of sin. It had to be demonstrated that God did not owe anything except judgment to any man. It had to be manifested that man could do nothing for himself and that permanent blessings could come only by grace on account of Christ.

In this sense Israel was God's people and the other nations were "no-peoples." God, of course, was the only true God. All others idols and god-ideas were and are demons. It would seem almost incredible that a people who had been the object of so much power and so much love could turn against the true God and insult Him by ascribing worship or praise to some stick, stone, or fetish. Yet, this they did, degenerating to the level of the peoples around them who had sunk into the degradation that devil worship brings. It was in such circumstances that God announced, "This people has stirred me to jealousy with what is a no-god, I will stir them to jealousy with a no-people."

With this understanding of the righteousness of true jealousy, we may return to the verse in Deuteronomy which is quoted in our text in Romans. "I will provoke you to jealousy with a no-people, and with a foolish nation will I anger you." The men of Israel in Paul's day had to be brought to understand that God's turning to the Gentiles and Paul's proclamation of free grace and full access to the God and Father of our Lord Jesus Christ, the God of Abraham, Isaac and Jacob, was in the fabric of the original plan of God. The fact that they had turned their eyes to a single facet of truth and had blindly supposed that there was no other truth was not pertinent to the argument. They had to be undeceived. They had to be brought to realize that they did not have any claim upon God in their own right. Everything that had ever been done for them was the result of the grace of God, and they were not to be astonished because grace went beyond them in the wider circle of God's love for the entire human race that was now being made manifest.

We who are Gentiles by birth must understand the implication of this text for us. We were a "no-people." No Gentile people can have any pride of ancestry that is worth anything. If we who are Gentiles must humbly accept our position as a "no-people" and come to God only through His grace, those who are of the original covenant people must also understand that God has their best interests in view. God says that He has chosen us who are Gentiles to enter into the new covenant relationship with Him in order to provoke His former chosen people to jealousy. He wants them to see that, temporarily, they have been supplanted. He wants them to realize that the veil in the temple has been torn in two and that there is no more priesthood, no more altar of sacrifice, and no more approach to God in the old ritual way. He wants them to know that the Messiah belongs, for this age, to a "no-people." He wants them to look at us, the "no-people," the foolish nation, and realize what blessings their fathers let slip so easily.

A Contrary People

Now we come to the end of Paul's great defense of God's methods of salvation by grace, and to the end of the presentation of the truth of the universality of the Gospel. "But Isaiah is very bold, and says, I was found of them that sought me not; I was made manifest to them that asked not after me. But to Israel he says, All day long I have held out my hands to a disobedient and contrary people" (Rom. 10:20, 21).

CHAPTER XI

From the beginning God had moved toward all of the human race. He had offered salvation to Adam and Eve and in their presence had made the first promise of the coming Savior who would bruise the head of Satan. God had told the story of the Gospel to Adam and had pegged it to the stars to help them remember. Moses had announced that a "no-people" would be saved and that a foolish nation would come to the truth.

The last witness who comes forward is Isaiah, the greatest of all the prophets of the Messiah. The quotation that Paul makes is from the sixty-fifth chapter of the prophecy. It should be noted, in the light of the attempts of critics to deny the authorship of the prophecy, that the Holy Spirit flatly says that Isaiah is the author of the last part of the book. If we have to choose between the critics and the Word of the Lord, we shall do well to remember the words of the old Scotch lady who said, sagely, "I have learned that in the long run, the Almighty is generally correct."

When we turn back to Isaiah and read the prophecy in several translations, we find some difference between versions as to the tense of the verbs. The King James Version reads, "I am sought of them that asked not for me; I am found of them that sought me not." The Revised Standard Version reads, "I was ready to be sought by those who did not ask for me; I was ready to be found by those who did not seek me." The translation made by Jewish scholars and published by the Jewish Publication Society of America reads, "I gave access to them that asked not for me; I was at hand to them that sought me not." In the footnotes to this same translation, the editors admit that literally the passage should read, "allowed myself to be enquired of by them, I let myself be found by them that sought me not."*

Here is a case where men have failed because there was no recognition of the spiritual meaning of the passage in the light of the New Testament. The passage in Isaiah, the Holy Spirit tells us in Romans, was a bold statement. In fact, Isaiah is said to have been very bold in announcing such a truth. He was as bold as a prophet in Moscow today would be if he announced before the Supreme Council of the Soviet Union that the American way of free enterprise was the only way that could succeed.

It is only natural that the bold declaration of Isaiah was not received by the people before whom he prophesied. We must never forget that most people are not controlled by reason. Unfortunate the man who thinks that if he prepares his thesis in cold logic, it will immediately batter down all resistance. The hearers too often do not hear with their reason but with their emotions. A logical argument will be presented and the hearer will take one phrase out of the argument, carry it over to a corner of his mind as a dog will take a bone, and worry it while the speaker goes on

---

* *The Holy Scriptures*, (*1917 Translation*), used by permission of The Jewish Publication Society, Philadelphia, Pa.

with the rest of the logical presentation. When the listener finally leaves the bone and comes back to the main line of the argument, he has hopelessly missed the train of thought. Thus it is that men are blinded by prejudice. We must not forget that the word *prejudice* is Latin for "judgment in advance." It was this judgment in advance which had blinded Israel. Their minds were so filled with the false idea that God could not work apart from them that they were simply blind and deaf to any suggestion that God was universal or that He would ever turn away from them and work with elements from other nations, whom they had learned to despise.

Isaiah quotes God as saying, "I have been found by those who did not seek me; I have shown myself to those who did not ask for me." In order to understand this fully we must remind ourselves of the state of the Gentile world at the time of the incarnation of our Lord Jesus Christ. We must rid our minds of preconceived notions. When He came the first time, He fulfilled Isaiah's bold words and was found of those who did not seek Him, and showed Himself to those who did not ask for Him.

We turn now to the second half of the quotation from Isaiah and read, "But of Israel he says, All day long I have held out my hand to a disobedient and contrary people." Yet we must not forget that this is the people of whom He had Moses sing, "Is not he your father, who created you, who made you and established you? . . . The Lord's portion is his people; Jacob his allotted heritage. He found him in a desert land, and in the howling waste of the wilderness he encircled him; he cared for him; he kept him as the apple of his eye. Like an eagle that stirs up its nest, that flutters over its young, spreading out its wings, catching them, bearing them on its pinions, the Lord alone did lead him, and there was no foreign god with him. He made him ride on the high places of the earth, and he ate the produce of the field, and he made him suck honey out of the rock, and oil out of the flinty rock. Curds from the herd, and milk from the flock, with fat of lambs and rams, herds of Bashan and goats, with the finest of the wheat—and of the blood of the grape, you drank wine" (Deut. 32:6, 9–14).

It is to this beloved people for which He had done everything that the Lord now stretches out His hand all the day long. Who is it that speaks? The Lord of glory. How does He describe Himself? As stretching out His hands. Have you ever stretched out your hands for five minutes? It begins to be painful. It would be absolutely impossible for any member of the human race to stretch out his hands for a whole day. Yet God, the Creator God, the Almighty God, describes Himself as stretching out His hands all the day long. Toward whom is He stretching out His hands? Toward the people whom He has loved so long and for whom He has done so much. His hands were (and are) held out toward a people who are described in the most terrible terms.

CHAPTER XI

At this point in my preparation I realized that this picture of God is to be found in the end of the prophecy of Isaiah. I turned back to the beginning of the prophecy and began to write down the description of the people as God had given it to Isaiah in the prophecies of judgment. Through Isaiah Israel is described as: a sinful nation, a hypocritical nation, a people laden with iniquity, rebellious sons, offspring of evildoers, corruptors, forsakers of the Lord, provokers of the Holy One of Israel, despisers of God, companions of thieves, wicked, wanton, rotten, drunken, bribegivers, bribe-takers, proud, arrogant, makers of evil laws, godless, oppressors, treacherous dealers, proud drunkards, filthy, and scornful men.

By the time I had written down the above in my notes, I was one-third of the way through the prophecy. Suddenly, as I was meditating on the horror of it all, I began to think that there are no terms or combination of terms in the human language which depict evil that may not be used in describing all men, as well as Israel, when out of the will of God. Apart from Jesus Christ, this is what we are. Yet God is holding out His arms all the day long to them. We can hear the sob of Christ if we listen closely, as He held out His arms, "O Jerusalem, Jerusalem, thou that killest the prophets and stonest them that are sent unto you, how often would I have gathered thee to my bosom as a hen gathereth her chicks, but ye would not!" (Matt. 23:37).

Rebellion

Throughout the Old Testament we find that the children of Israel scorned the men who brought them the blessings of God and the offers of grace. God called Abraham, who wanted God to bless through Ishmael instead of Isaac. He wanted his own way instead of God's. Isaac tried to get out of God's way in order to bless Esau instead of Jacob. Eleven of the twelve sons of Jacob tried to murder Joseph because he had been chosen of God for a specific purpose.

Moses discovered the heart of this people as soon as he started out to fulfill the plan of God. By the time the host of Israel had reached the edge of the Red Sea, and before they had passed over, the people wanted to refuse the grace of God and return to slavery and their own lusts. We read, "And they said to Moses, Is it because there are no graves in Egypt that you have taken us away to die in the wilderness? What have you done to us in bringing us out of Egypt? Is this not what we said to you in Egypt. Let us alone and let us serve the Egyptians?" (Exod. 14:11, 12). Later they cried out that Moses had gone too far. Korah and his group came to Moses, saying, "You take too much upon you . . . Why do you exalt yourself above the assembly of the Lord?" (Num. 16:3). When Jeremiah came and preached to the people, they said, "As for the word which you have spoken to us in the name of the Lord, we will not listen to you" (Jer. 44:16). Ezekiel was called upon to warn the bloody city but when he had finished his warning, he I said, "O, Lord God, they are saying of me; is he not speaking parables?" (Ezek. 20:49). A very modern translation might render it, "Isn't he talking through his hat?"

Amos preached the truth throughout the land of Israel and Amaziah, the false priest, who had set up the demon altar at Bethel, went to the king and said, "Amos has conspired against you in the midst of the house of Israel; the land is not able to bear all his words." This same Amaziah then said to the prophet of God, "O seer, go, flee away to the land of Judah and eat bread there and prophesy there; but never again prophesy at Bethel, for it is the king's sanctuary; it is the temple of the kingdom" (Amos 7:10–13).

Hatred for Christ

The Lord Jesus Christ Himself was received with the same hatred. He summed it all up in the mighty parable of the householder. "There was a householder who planted a vineyard, and set a hedge around it, and dug a wine press in it, and built a tower, and let it out to tenants, and went into another country. When the season of fruit drew near, he sent his servants to the tenants to get his fruit; the tenants took his servants and beat one, killed another, and stoned another. Again he sent other servants, more than the first; and they did the same to them. Afterward he sent his son to them, saying, 'They will respect my son.' When the tenants saw the son, they said to themselves, 'This is the heir; come, let us kill him and have his inheritance.' They took him and cast him out of the vineyard and killed him. When therefore the owner of the vineyard comes, what will he do to those tenants? They said to him [Jesus], 'He will put those wretches to a miserable death, and let out the vineyard to other tenants who will give him the fruits in their seasons.' Jesus said to them, 'Have you never read in the scriptures: "The very stone which the builders rejected has become the head of the corner; this was the Lord's doing, and it is marvelous in our eyes?" Therefore I tell you, the kingdom of God will be taken away from you and given to a nation producing the fruits of it'" (Matt. 21:33–43).

The Lord God is the householder. His earth is the vineyard. The children of Israel were the tenants. The prophets were the Lord's agents who came to turn them to God. The martyrdom of the prophets is the beating of the servants. The Lord Jesus Christ is the Son who was sent in the last instance. The rebellion against Christ is the rebellion against the Son. The crucifixion was the death of the Son. The casting of Israel out of Palestine and the destruction of Jerusalem is the judgment upon the wicked servants. The Gentile believers are the nation bringing forth the fruits. In the eleventh chapter we will see in what danger we Gentile believers stand.

We cannot leave this final picture of the patient God without pointing out to all men, Jew and Gentile alike, that the Lord still stands with outstretched arms, calling men to Himself. Take it in the words of God as He stood here on earth, "Come to me, all who labor and are heavy laden and I will give you rest. Take my yoke upon you and learn from me; for I am gentle and lowly in heart and you will find rest for your souls. My yoke is easy and my burden is light" (Matt. 11:28–30). Let us turn to the very last paragraph in the Bible. Here we will find God stretching out His arms to men that they might come to Him for life. "The Spirit and the Bride say, Come. Let him who hears, say, Come. Let him who is thirsty come. Let everyone who desires to take the water of life without price" (Rev. 22:17).

XII

The People of the Promise

"I say then, Has God cast off his people? God forbid. For I also am an Israelite, of the seed of Abraham, of the tribe of Benjamin. God has not cast away his people which he foreknew. Do you not know what the Scripture says of Elias? how he maketh intercession to God against Israel, saying, Lord, they have killed thy prophets, and digged down thine altars; and I am left alone, and they seek my life. But what says the answer of God unto him? I have reserved to myself seven thousand men, who have not bowed the knee to the image of Baal. Even so then at this present time also there is a remnant according to the election of grace. And if by grace, then is it no more of works: otherwise grace is no more grace. But if it be of works, then is it no more grace: otherwise work is no more work" (Rom. 11:1–6).

The question immediately arises, "Has God cast off His people?" The answer is in the same words that Paul uses to answer other follies that people bring forth against the truth of God. "God forbid!" Other translations render it, "Never," "Far from it," "By no means."

As we go on through the chapter, we shall come more and more to see that there are hundreds of promises to Israel as a nation which have not yet been fulfilled and that they must be fulfilled to the last detail. Our text may not be interpreted to read as nothing more than a statement that Christ is the door for the Jews as well as Gentiles. As far as I am concerned, if God does not bring the Jews back into Palestine and give them the whole of the land, Jordan as well as Israel, Syria, Lebanon, and much of the Near East, then the Bible is not a trustworthy book.

CHAPTER XII

The Testimony of Israel

I recall an anecdote which I heard as a student. I am not able to verify the source, but the force of the story will carry it without verification. It would appear that about a hundred years ago the King of Prussia was having a discussion with his chaplain on the veracity of the Bible. The king said to the chaplain, "Give me in a word proof that the Bible is the inspired Word of God." The chaplain replied, "Your Majesty, it is possible for me to answer your request with great literality. I can give you proof in one single word that the Bible is the Word of God."

The king looked at him in amazement and said, "What is this magic word which carries such a weight of proof with it?" The chaplain replied, "Your Majesty, that word is *Israel*." He was right, of course. There are other single words which also prove the Bible—sin, salvation, Christ—but the history of the people of Israel is sufficient to show that a divine breath came upon the men who held the pens that wrote down the Word of God.

It must be specifically noted that in the thirteenth verse of this chapter Paul states that he is addressing this portion of his argument to the Gentiles. In the city of Rome, there were many Christians. Many of them, like the disciples themselves, had been Jews. The church at Rome had been founded by merchant Jews who happened to be on a visit to Palestine at the time of Christ's death and the events of Pentecost. The book of the Acts records their presence in Jerusalem (2:10). These Jews had returned to their homes in Rome, and had met together for the breaking of bread and the fellowship of the new faith. Paul was very conscious of the fact that the assembly of believers in Rome was made up of two groups with different backgrounds—of Jews who knew all the lore of the rabbis and of Gentiles who had come out of paganism, knowing nothing whatsoever of Moses and the religion that had been twisted out of his teachings by the Pharisees. Paul had spoken in earlier portions of the epistle to first one of these groups, then the other, and then to both together. Now, he directly addresses himself to the Gentiles.

Israel's place

You Gentiles have been brought into the church of Jesus Christ. Does this mean that God has cast off His ancient people? It is true that God has changed His methods of dealing with men so that it is no longer necessary to approach Him through the sacrifices of Israel. Since the Lamb of God died to take away the sin of the world (John 1:29), there is no more place for the lambs of God. God is through with the altar, the priesthood, and the Temple. God now lives in the hearts of those men who are made partakers of the divine nature in the new birth. He will no longer use any building as His dwelling place. Because He is through with the Temple, He is not, in this age at least, exclusively interested in Palestine. Because there have been all these changes, does it mean that we are to go one step further and say that God is through with the people whom He chose? God forbid. The process stops there. For God has not cast off His people forever; He has a definite place for them in His eternal plan.

How many times in the Old Testament did He tell them again that He would never forsake them? He would chastise them, by sending against them other nations who would whip them like scorpions, plow their cities, and carry the people captive, but He would not forsake them. They would go through periods when they would be ridiculed by all other nations, but God would never forsake them. There would even be a time when God would call them "not my people" and "not pitied," but He would not forsake them; He would ultimately bring them back to Himself.

Not Forsaken

At the moment when the people asked Samuel to give them a king in order that they might be like the nations around them, Samuel knew that the request was a great sin. Asking for a king was equivalent to asking to be ruled by a man instead of God alone. In the moment of their great sin, Samuel said to them, "Fear not, you who have done all this wickedness . . . for the Lord will not forsake his people for his great name's sake, because it has pleased the Lord to make you his people" (1 Sam. 12:20, 22).

In the Psalms we read the inspired cry of anguish that goes up from a singer because the people of God are being broken by the enemy. David points out that the enemy thinks that God has forgotten His people and that the God of Jacob is no longer looking after them. Then he sings, "The Lord knows the thoughts of man, that they are but a breath" (Ps. 94:11). He is enabled to continue in triumph, "Blessed is the man whom thou dost chasten, O Lord, and whom thou dost teach out of thy law to give him rest from days of trouble until the pit is dug for the wicked. For the Lord will not cast off his people; he will not forsake his inheritance" (Ps. 94:12–14).

Nehemiah recounts the history of the people by recalling that they had been faithful to God until they became prosperous, but that in prosperity they had departed from God. He would send enemies to hurt them but, as soon as the people got rested from the hurt of one punishment, they would go their own way again. We read, "Nevertheless they were disobedient and rebelled against thee and cast thy law behind their backs and killed thy prophets, who had warned them in order to turn them back to thee, and they committed great blasphemies. Therefore thou didst give them into the hand of their enemies, who made them suffer; and in the time of their suffering they cried to thee and thou didst hear them from heaven; and according to thy great mercies thou didst give them saviors who saved them from the hand of their enemies. But after they had rest they did evil again before thee, and thou didst abandon them to the hand of their enemies so that they had dominion over them; yet when they turned and cried to thee, thou didst hear from heaven, and many times thou didst deliver them according to thy mercies. And thou didst warn them in order to turn them back to thy law. Yet they acted presumptuously and did not obey thy commandments but sinned against thy ordinances by the observance of which a man shall live, and turned a stubborn shoulder and stiffened their neck and would not obey. Many years thou didst bear with them and didst warn them by thy Spirit through thy prophets; yet they would not give ear. Therefore thou didst give them into the hand of the peoples of the lands" (Neh. 9:26–30).

Not Utterly Consumed

It would have appeared many times that they had been cast off by God but He had not cast them off. It might have seemed to them that they had been forsaken by God but the next verse tells us the whole story: "Nevertheless for thy great mercies' sake thou didst not utterly consume them nor forsake them; for thou art a gracious and merciful God" (v. 31). Consumed, but not utterly consumed—that was the history of Israel throughout the Old Testament, and Paul is announcing here in Romans 11 that there has not been any change in God's methods or in God's final objective. He still must show His righteousness by chastening those who forsake Him, but He will still be gracious to a remnant whom He will choose as the objects of His mercy.

Listen to Isaiah. The great fifty-third chapter tells us of the death and resurrection of the Lord Jesus Christ. Immediately we hear in the fifty-fourth chapter: "Sing, O barren, thou that didst not bear; break forth into singing, and cry aloud, thou that didst not travail with child . . . For thou shalt break forth on the right hand and on the left, and thy descendants shall possess the nations and make the desolate cities to be inhabited. Fear not, for thou shat not be ashamed; neither be thou confounded, for thou shalt not be put to shame . . . For a small moment have I forsaken thee; but with great mercies will I gather thee. In a little wrath I hid my face from thee for a moment; but with everlasting kindness will I have mercy on thee, saith the Lord thy Redeemer" (Isa. 54:1–8). God goes on to say that His dealings with Israel have been like the waters of Noah. These waters passed over the earth once, but, says God, "As I have sworn that the waters of Noah should no more go over the earth, so have I sworn that I would not be wroth [with Israel] nor rebuke

[Israel]. For the mountains shall depart, and the hills be removed, but my kindness shall not depart from thee, neither shall the covenant of my peace be removed, saith the Lord that hath mercy on thee" (Isa. 54:9, 10). Then the Lord comforts His people. Some day the following words will penetrate into the hearts of the nation which He chose and which is forsaken for the "small moment" and pursued with the "little wrath," "O thou afflicted, tossed with tempest, and not comforted, behold I will lay thy stones with fair colors and lay thy foundations with sapphires ... And all thy children shall be taught of the Lord and great shall be the peace of thy children. In righteousness shalt thou be established; thou shalt be far from oppression, thou shalt not fear; thou shalt be far from terror, for it shall not come near thee ... No weapon that is formed against thee shall prosper, and every tongue that shall rise against thee in judgment thou shalt condemn. This is the heritage of the servants of the Lord, and their righteousness is of me, saith the Lord" (Isa. 54:11, 13, 14, 17).

Paul was steeped in the Old Testament. Its promises were in his heart. We can well understand his horror at the thought that all these promises made to the nation of Israel might be taken as though they were the words of a man. "I say then, Has God cast off His people? God forbid!" Has God become a man that He should lie? Has God become a promise breaker? Have justice, righteousness and honor departed from the Deity?

Paul's Testimony

Paul's first proof of the fact that God has not cast off Israel is himself. He outlines his own place in the covenant. He says, "For I myself am an Israelite, a descendant of Abraham, a member of the tribe of Benjamin."

"I am an Israelite." He was writing to the church in Rome where there were both those of the physical seed of Abraham and Gentile proselytes to Judaism. It is interesting to note that the Holy Spirit records a list of some of the nations present in Jerusalem on the day of Pentecost. It speaks of nationals from many nations, mentioning fourteen by name. When it comes to the description of those from the capitol of the world, it says, "visitors from Rome, both Jews and proselytes" (Acts 2:10). Paul is going to make very sure that they do not think that he is one of these proselytes. He was not a Gentile by birth. He had been born in a Gentile country where his own people were a small minority, but he was a Jew and very proud of it. "I am an Israelite," he says, "a descendant of Abraham."

He then notes that he is of the tribe of Benjamin. There had been a civil war in Israel after the death of Solomon and ten of the tribes had separated themselves from Judah and Benjamin. They had withdrawn into the north and had refused to come to Jerusalem to offer the blood sacrifices. They had apostatized and set up schismatic altars. They had created an alien priesthood and had built temples at both Bethel and Gilgal. These may have been places with deep religious memories in the history of the people of God; but after He had set up the sacrifices at Jerusalem, God pronounced a curse on anyone who would offer a sacrifice for sin anywhere in the world except at the door of the tabernacle of the Lord (Lev. 17:1–9), Paul wants the Gentiles in Rome to realize that he is an Israelite and that he does not come from one of the ten tribes which had done these terrible things. He was a child of Benjamin, the tribe which had remained with Judah. Benjamin was the smallest of the tribes, Saul reminds us when he is chosen to be king (1 Sam. 9:21). David describes it as "little Benjamin" (Ps. 68:27). When Moses was about to die, he blessed the tribes and gave to Benjamin the most spiritual of all the blessings. Of Benjamin he said, "The beloved of the Lord shall dwell in safety by him; and the Lord shall cover him all the day long, and he shall dwell between his shoulders" (Deut. 33:12).

When Paul cries out that he is of the tribe of Benjamin, he is giving a boast that is filled with proper pride. He has indeed been blessed by the Lord. Has God cast Paul off? God forbid. He is a real Israelite from the smallest tribe, a tribe to which God has promised great blessings. Paul is not going to be denied his place in the fulfillment of those promises.

The idea that God could have broken His promises, changed His mind, and cast off the people whom He had chosen for Himself was thoroughly repugnant to Paul, the apostle. His first argument, after his exclamation of horror at the idea, was that he himself was an Israelite, of the descendants of Abraham and of the tribe of Benjamin.

His second argument goes back into the nature of God, His sovereignty, and His choice of the people. It is a flat statement. God has not rejected His people whom He foreknew.

Sovereign Grace

Once more we emphasize that God's foreknowledge cannot mean mere advance knowledge. The moment we speak of foreknowledge in God, we speak of eternal purpose and divine ordination that a thing shall come to pass. William Kelly has well pointed out that the Bible does not speak of "a passive or naked foreknowledge, as if God only saw beforehand what someone would be, do, or believe. His foreknowledge is of persons, not of their state or conduct; it is not *what* but *whom* He foreknew."

Thus it is that Paul is able to make such a flat, categorical statement. "God has not cast away his people whom he foreknew." God is not fickle. God does not change. In Him there is no change, nor could there be. Since this people is everywhere spoken of as His eternal choice, there can be no question of God's moving away from His eternal course. Before the chapter is over, we will hear Paul say, "The gifts and calling of God are without repentance" (v. 29). The Revised Standard Version gives us a much stronger translation: "The gifts and the call of God are irrevocable." When God gives something, by the very nature of His being, He cannot take it back. When God sets a plan, by the very nature of His being, He cannot change that plan. We will find that from time to time He opens a parenthesis in His dealings with men and pursues a plan within a plan, but He will return to His original promises and will follow through with His original plan. God will never be frustrated. Everthing He has planned will surely come to pass.

God has preserved for Himself a remnant. There was no reason within the people themselves for God to have preserved any portion of them. All had come under the righteous judgment of God, but grace manifested itself because God is a faithful God. In order to make his argument stronger, Paul adds that the remnant that was saved was not only saved through grace but that it was the elective grace of God. Once more we are carried back into the heart of God and given a look at the fact that He has an eternal purpose. Our present text cannot be understood without reading into it what has been said in the ninth chapter of this epistle. All who were being saved, whether from the world of Israel or from among the Gentiles, were being saved by the sovereign choice of God, purely on the grounds of His grace. Paul proceeds to amplify, once more, the nature of grace. "If by grace, then it is no more of works: otherwise grace is no more grace." The Revised Standard Version stops at this point and leaves out the last half of the verse because the majority of the manuscripts stop at this point. A strong minority of the manuscripts, however, restate the argument in another form as we have it in the King James Version. The argument, indeed, is complete if we stop at the end of the first half of the verse, but it is well to consider the restatement also: "But if it be of works, then it is no more grace; otherwise work is no more work." John Owen, who translated Calvin's commentaries into English more than one hundred years ago, says in his footnote on this passage, "This kind of statement is wholly in unison with the apostle's mode of writing. He often states a thing positively and negatively or in two different ways. (Compare Romans 4:5; 9:1; Eph. 2:8, 9). Then an *omission* is more probable than an *addition*... Every reason except the number of manuscripts is in favor of its genuineness." I shall in this case follow the minority of the manuscripts and retain the last half of the verse, although I repeat, the argument is complete without its inclusion. It is well, on a point as important as the nature of salvation and the relationship of grace and works, to say the matter twice. We can drive the nail through the board and then turn the board over to clinch the nail.

CHAPTER XII

Our text is the simplest expression of elementary mathematics. If a debt has been entirely paid, there is nothing left to be paid. If you have a debt of one hundred dollars and your brother offers to pay the debt for you and presents you with a receipt for the full amount, you are no more obligated to the creditor. The debt has been fully satisfied. No part of it can henceforth be levied against you. If the Lord Jesus Christ paid for the full guilt of our sin, there is no guilt left to be paid for in any other fashion. There is no verse in the Bible that says that repentance pays for sin, that subsequent works pay for sin, or that baptism or any other religious act pays for sin. There are many verses which show us that the blood of Jesus Christ, God's Son, cleanses from all sin (1 John 1:7).

We return now to the main theme of our text in Romans. Because salvation is by grace, works have no part in it. The reason that this is true is that works have originated within the heart of man. They have their spring in the heart of that which has come from Adam. The whole idea of works is that man can provide a basis to force God to give him some blessings as a just reward for the works. The whole idea of grace is that God acts toward man entirely according to that which is to be found within His own divine nature of love. The two ideas are mutually exclusive and destroy each other when placed together.

From time to time I meet with men who say to me that they want God to be just to them and that they can rely on His justice to give them what they deserve. I cry out at once that they are fools. I point out to them that if God dealt with them on the basis of His justice, they would receive the judgment of His holy wrath. God's holiness cannot tolerate sin, nor will it permit Him to allow the sinner in His presence. If I were to receive the justice of God, that justice would demand that I must go to hell. It was the justice of God that struck down the Lord Jesus Christ when He was on the cross. It is now possible for me to run to the cross and to hide myself in the Rock that was cleft for my refuge. His mercy and grace is now my portion which shields me from the wrath which His holy justice demands for sinners. Because the death of the Lord Jesus Christ on the cross satisfies the demands of justice, I am bound for heaven, a victim of His love and grace. Such love calls forth the gratitude of my heart and causes me to walk in those good works "which God hath before ordained that we should walk in them" (Eph. 2:10).

XIII

When God Hardens Hearts

What then? Israel failed to obtain that which he seeks for. But the elect obtained it, and the rest were hardened (as it is written, "God gave them a spirit of stupor, eyes that should not see and ears that should not hear,) down to this very day." And David says, "Let their table be made a snare and a trap, a pitfall and a retribution for them; let their eyes be darkened so that they cannot see, and bend their backs forever (Rom. 11:7–10).

Having established that God has not cast off His people, we then ask, What is their true position? It certainly appears that they have been cast off, but man looks on the outward appearance and the Lord sees the inwardness of reality. God did not push Israel away; God has never pushed any man away. It was true then as it is true today; if we draw nigh to God; He will draw nigh to us (Jas. 4:8). Any man who is away from God is where he is because of his own desires. Man cut himself off from God when Adam sinned, and every man who is still outside of God in Christ is there because he cuts himself off from God and pushes himself away from the truth.

Israel's Failure

First, we are told that Israel failed to obtain that for which it was seeking. We are told elsewhere that Israel was seeking after righteousness. We have already seen that they had a zeal for God but that it was not according to knowledge. They were ignorant of the righteousness that comes from God and, as they were trying to establish their own righteousness, they did not submit to the righteousness of God (10:2, 3). We have seen that their own Scriptures showed the way of righteousness but that they were not willing to accept it. If they had called on the name of the Lord, they would have been saved, but they were so proud of their own efforts that they would not stoop to take things in God's way. God pointed down to Christ as to a lowly stone lying on the ground despised and rejected by men, but a stone whom He intended to make the head of the corner. They looked away from the ground and stumbled over the stone. It was their failure to accept the fact that the way to God's righteousness is by the recognition of human bankruptcy and the declaration of total dependency on the substitute Saviour that led them far from God.

It must be understood also that the national life of Israel was entirely concerned with the concept of obtaining righteousness. Their law concerned righteousness. Their religious observances concerned ceremonial righteousness. They thought that the ceremonial washing of pots and pans and the ceremonial washing of their hands could fulfill the requirements of divine righteousness. It was thus that Israel failed to obtain that which it sought.

The Remnant—and the Rest

But in the midst of the whole nation that was seeking righteousness through the law, there was a small remnant that God chose to find righteousness through grace. If God had not proceeded through divine sovereignty to choose a remnant, there would not have been any saved at all. We must never forget this fact. If we are saved, it is because of God's grace and not because of anything that was in us.

Now if the elected remnant obtained the righteousness for which the others were seeking what happened to the majority? God's answer is direct. They were hardened. If you are tempted to cry out against God at this point, remember His scathing rebuke to all who fight this truth. We saw it in chapter nine: "Who are you, a man, to answer back to God?" (9:20). Rather, come in all humility and ask the question that will also search your own soul. That question is: If men are judicially blinded or hardened, how and why does this take place?

We should note, first, that the original language does not say "blinded," but "hardened." I cannot understand why the translators of the King James Version used the word "blinded." The Greek word is one that means to cover with a thick skin. Their hearts and minds have been covered over with scar tissue. They have lost the sap out of their wood and have become petrified.

Hearts Hardened

This is the same word that is used in Second Corinthians to describe the inability of any child of Israel to understand the Old Testament. We read, "Since we have such a hope, we are very bold, not like Moses, who put a veil over his face so that the Israelites might not see the end of the fading splendor. But their minds were hardened; for to this day, when they read the old covenant, that same veil remains unlifted, because only through Christ is it taken away. Yes, to this day whenever Moses is read a veil lies over their minds; but when a man turns to the Lord the veil is removed" (2 Cor. 3:12–16). If we take this passage and weave it into the one we are studying in Romans, we will learn much more about the process by which men allow themselves to be hardened. Be assured that when we read that God hardened their hearts the Bible is not saying that God arbitrarily and maliciously makes men into unbelievers. Such an idea is alien to all that the Word of God teaches us about God the Father of our Lord Jesus Christ. We must not forget either that God is a God of holiness and that He must work according to the laws of His inner nature. Sin came originally from Satan and human sin from Adam, but God has made all the rules under which sin shall be committed. If men will leave God's flowing spring and willfully march into swamp, the law of the sucking quicksand will come into effect. If men will leave God's flowing spring and willfully march into the desert, the law of thirst will come into effect. If men will leave God's will and way and walk after their own way, the law of the hardening of the heart will come into effect.

It is of great importance that we examine this process of hardening because there are multitudes in our day who are walking in paths of willfulness and being hardened because of a misuse of the blessings which God has given them. If we look closely at the hardening of Israel in ancient times, it is because we wish to draw warnings and lessons for our own hearts and for the hearts of others in our day. We must not forget that God has told us that "these things happened to them as a warning, but they were written down for our instruction, upon whom the end of the ages has come. Therefore let any one who thinks that he stands take heed lest he fall" (1 Cor. 10:11, 12).

Paul now introduces, under the guidance and inspiration of the Holy Spirit, a tissue of quotations from the Old Testament to show how the hardening process came to Israel. It is important to notice how the Holy Spirit can take a line from Isaiah, a line from Deuteronomy, and a line from the Psalms, put them all together and present a conclusive argument. It is the same method that was used in the third chapter of Romans where the whole development of wickedness is traced through the anatomy of the human body.

Author's Rights

Some critics have been disturbed because the quotations are not letter for letter the same as written in the original passages of the Old Testament. They forget that the Holy Spirit is the author of the epistle to the Romans just as He is the author of the prophecy of Isaiah, the Psalms of David, and all the rest of Scripture. When an author wishes to refer to something he has said in another place, he reserves the right to shorten, amplify, or paraphrase. If human authors are thus sovereign over their previous writings, let us not deny to the Lord God Almighty the right to deal with His Word as He pleases. The Hebrew of Isaiah 29:10, 11, of which a part is first quoted here, reads: "For the Lord has poured out upon you a spirit of deep sleep and has closed your eyes, the prophets, and covered your heads, the seers. And the vision of all this has become to you like the words of a book that is sealed." The Septuagint translation reads, "The Lord has made you drink of the spirit of deep sleep." Whether this spirit of stupor was poured upon them or whether they drank it, most certainly it came from God because of their departure from Him.

The reason for this hardening is given in the next paragraph. "Because this people draw near with their mouth and honor me with their lips, while their hearts are far from me and their fear of me is a commandment of men learned by rote; therefore, behold, I will again do marvelous things with this people, wonderful and marvelous; the wisdom of their wise men shall perish and the discernment of their discerning men shall be hid" (Isa. 29:13, 14).

Departure from God

It can be seen that the hardening of their hearts by God was the result of their departure from God. We would disagree violently with Calvin at this point. He turns the whole argument around and tries to make it read that the people departed because God had willfully hardened them. There is no such teaching in the Word of God.

The second part of the quotation comes from an earlier chapter in Isaiah. The prophet had seen a vision of the Lord and immediately knew that he, himself, was a man of unclean lips and that he dwelt in the midst of a people of unclean lips (Isa. 6:5). When he was cleansed, the Lord sent him to prophesy to the people, saying, "Hear and hear, but do not understand; see and see, but do not perceive" (v. 9). Again we note that the hardening was because the people had departed from the Lord and had become a people of unclean lips.

The quotation continues and shifts now to the Psalms. In one of the foremost of the Messianic Psalms, we read of the rejection of the Messiah and of God's judgment upon the people because of that rejection. "Let their own table before them become a snare; let their sacrificial feasts be a trap. Let their eyes be darkened so that they cannot see and make their loins tremble continually" (Ps. 69:22, 23).

When God Hardens Hearts

The significance of the whole judgment can now be seen. God had given to Israel a place of close fellowship which they had abandoned for strange gods. David could sing, "Thou preparest a table before me in the presence of my enemies" (Ps. 23:5). That table had become a snare. God had given them the altar of sacrifice for the remission of their sins and it had become a trap for them.

Blessing Cursed

There is a great illustration of this in the book of Malachi. In one of the most tragic passages in the entire Bible we read, "And now, O priests, this command is for you. If you will not listen, if you will not lay it to heart to give glory to my name, says the Lord of hosts, then I will send the curse upon you and I will curse your blessings; indeed I have already cursed them because you do not lay it to heart" (Mal. 2:1, 2).

What a tragedy this is! The curse of blessings is probably the worst of all curses. The things that should have brought men nearer to God finally take them farther away from God. We have an illustration of this in our own national life. When MacArthur and our troops entered Japan, they took control of the archives of the Japanese war department. Men were set to work to translate all the enemy papers. They discovered that in the years previous to the war, the Japanese had sent their most eminent professors of psychology to every part of the United States to make a study of our national character in order to determine at what point we would be most vulnerable to attack. The combined reports concluded that early on a Sunday morning following a Friday on which both the Army and the Navy got paid our guard would be the lowest. In former years Sunday was the day of our national rest. It was our blessing; God cursed it. The Japanese concluded that it had become the day of the national hangover. A friend of mine in Washington who has seen the yet unpublished report of the investigation concerning Pearl Harbor tells me that it states conclusively that the weekend of Pearl Harbor was the greatest debauch the islands had ever seen. Both the Army and the Navy had been paid on Friday. By Sunday morning our national blessing had been cursed and we had no proper defence available against the striking enemy.

Far greater than the curse of blessings that does no more than result in the bombing or the loss of a city is the curse of blessings which results in the eternal loss of souls. What shall it profit a man if he gain the whole world and lose his own soul? (Matt. 16:26). The blessings which God curses through Malachi are the blessings of the priest's high feasts. It is quite proper, therefore, that the modern translators of the Psalms should render the Hebrew word for "security," which reads "welfare" in the King James Version, as "Let their sacrificial feasts be a trap."

CHAPTER XIII

The Communion Table

I am afraid there are many people in our day and generation for whom the Lord's table is a snare and a trap. How terrible it is for an individual to go to the Lord's Supper and think that he is in a place of special privilege when he has no true fellowship with the Lord God who is the only giver of blessings! Must it not be said of many today, "Let their table be made a snare?" The Communion table is not to be the table of just any professing Christian; it is the Lord's table. No man has the right to close that table to anyone who wishes to come. The Lord even gave the bread and the cup to Judas, as is proved in the Gospel according to Luke where the two sentences are put in such close union that there can be no doubt. The Lord gave them the cup, saying, "This cup is the new covenant in my blood, which is shed for you; but, behold, the hand of him that betrayed me is with me on the table" (Luke 22:20, 21).

The table can be a snare that hardens the heart and makes a man think that he has satisfied God's demands for inward justice and righteousness because he has allied himself with the outward rites of some form of the Christian religion.

The same argument holds for the observance of the high festivals of Christendom. How many there are who observe Christmas, Lent and Easter and think that thereby they have satisfied the demands of God! Their festivals have become a trap for them. I do not expand on this because this particular portion of the quotation from the Psalms is omitted in our text in Romans.

The People to Blame

The quotation now shifts to the sixth of Isaiah which is quoted in four different places in the New Testament, each time with a slightly different emphasis. We have given the passage as it is found in Isaiah. The first time that it is quoted in the New Testament is by Jesus on the day that He first spoke in parables. The blame is put squarely upon the people themselves. We read, "You shall indeed hear but never understand, and you shall indeed see but never perceive. For this people's heart has grown dull, and their ears are heavy of hearing and their eyes they have closed, lest they should perceive with their eyes, and hear with their ears, and understand with their heart, and turn for me to heal them" (Matt. 13:14, 15). Here Christ points out that their sin caused their hardening.

At the end of our Lord's ministry, we find Him quoting these words again. Now there is a terrible change in the wording. It is no longer they who have closed their eyes and ears, but God. We read, "For Isaiah again said, He has blinded their eyes and hardened their heart, lest they should see with their eyes and perceive with their heart, and turn for me to heal them" (John. 12:39, 40). All of this goes to show that when man closes his eyes and ears to God he is in danger of having God further close them so that they cannot be opened.

Our present text is the third quotation of this text. Here the transition is being shown. The people departed from God; their hearts hardened; and God continued this hardening process until ultimately the people must be set aside.

The fourth time that this passage is quoted from Isaiah is in the last chapter of the Acts of the Apostles. The early missionary effort has been concluded. The church is well established and on its way. The judgments of God on Israel have been put into execution. Shortly before his death, the leaders of Israel in Rome gathered together in Paul's lodgings in great numbers. He expounded the whole gospel story unto them from morning until evening, testifying to the kingdom of God and trying to convince them about Jesus both from the law of Moses and from the prophets, Some were convinced by what he said, while others disbelieved. Paul made a closing statement before they departed. "The Holy Spirit was right in saying to your fathers through Isaiah the prophet, Go to this people and say, You shall indeed hear but never understand, and you shall indeed see but never perceive. For this people's heart has grown dull, and their ears are heavy of hearing, and their eyes they have closed; lest they should perceive with their eyes, and hear with their ears, and understand with their heart, and turn for me to heal them. Let it be known to you then that this salvation of God has been sent to the Gentiles; they will listen" (Acts 28:25–28). This has been God's word to Israel for the last nineteen centuries. He will not speak unto them again until the Lord Jesus comes the second time.

William R. Newell has an admirable footnote on this passage. He writes, "Since this awful use of Isaiah 6, the gospel has no Jewish bounds or bonds whatever! It is presumption and danger, now, to give the Jews any other place than that of common sinners! 'No distinction between Jew and Greek,' says God. Those who preach thus have God's blessing. Those that would give any special place whatever to Jews, since that day, do so contrary to the gospel; and, we fear, for private advantage. Tell the Jews *the truth*! Their Messiah *was* offered to their nation, and *rejected*. And God is *not offering a Messiah to Israel now*, but has Himself rejected them; all except a 'remnant,' who leave Jewish earthly hopes, break down into *sinners only*, and receive a sinner's Savior,—not a 'Jewish' one! Then they become 'partakers of a Heavenly calling'"*

---

* W. R. Newell, *Romans Verse by Verse*, used by permission of Moody Bible Institute and Moody Press, Chicago, Ill.

XIV

Israel's Future Glory

So I ask, have they stumbled so as to fall? By no means! But through their fall salvation has come to the Gentiles, so as to make Israel jealous. Now if their fall means riches for the world, and if their diminishing means riches for the Gentiles, how much more will their fullness mean? Now I speak to you that are Gentile. Inasmuch as I am the Apostle to the Gentiles, I magnify my office in order to turn some of my fellow Jews to emulation, and thus save some of them. For if their rejection means the reconciliation of the world, what will their acceptance mean but life from the dead? (Rom. 11:11–15).

Having set forth in the strongest language all that the Old Testament uses to describe the sin and judgment of Israel, Paul asks if the nation has stumbled so as to fall. He answers the question with the same indignation as he answered in the first verse. God has not cast away His people, and their fall is not a final fall. They have been set aside in order to allow God to pursue His greater and wider purpose. His promises to them are not conditional, and every word that He has spoken to them will be fulfilled.

Gentiles Adopted

God then sets forth the great fact that salvation is come to the Gentiles through their fall. We must not forget that before the time of Christ no Gentile could be saved unless he changed his nationality and became an integral part of Israel. It was necessary for a man to be circumcised and to be adopted into one of the tribes of Israel. Only then could he go beyond the wall of partition that kept the Gentiles far away from the sacred courts of the Lord. Only then could he bring a lamb and have the priests of the sons of Aaron shed the sacrificial blood that could cleanse him from his sins.

There are three outstanding examples of this in the Old Testament. When Naomi decided to return home to Palestine from the land of Moab after her sons had died, one of her daughters-in-law, Ruth the Moabitess, determined to accompany her. When Naomi sought to dissuade her, Ruth replied, in one of the most beautiful passages in the Bible, "Intreat me not to leave thee or to return from following after thee; for whither thou goest I will go, and whither thou lodgest I will lodge; thy people shall be my people and thy God my God" (Ruth 1:16). Note the order of the thought. She could not say, "Thy God shall be my God," until she had first said, "Thy people shall be my people." The change of nationality had to precede the change of God.

Again, when Naaman the Syrian came to the place of his salvation, it was first necessary for him to approach God as a Jew. When he first arrived in Palestine to ask healing from Elisha, he spurned the thought of dipping seven times in the Jordan, considering that river as contemptuous in comparison with the rivers of Damascus. After he had been healed, he did a thing that seems very strange if it is not understood theologically. He who had despised Palestinian water now ordered that two mule loads of earth be given to him. Why this sudden desire for Palestinian dirt? It was earth from the land of Israel and the explanation is to be found in the conjunction that joins the two halves of the sentence. "Let there be given to your servant two mules' burden of earth; *because* [that is the key word]—because henceforth your servant will not offer burnt offering or sacrifice to any god but to Jehovah" (2 Kings 5:17). We can see him returning to his house, cured. His family was in joy but his first care was to see that the sacks of dirt were carried into his house and carefully spread in a certain place. Then, whenever he wanted to pray, he would go and stand on this earth from the land of Israel, approaching God not as a Gentile, but on the ground of the covenant of promise.

The heart of the book of Esther shows this same great truth. With Haman hanged and Mordecai exalted, the Jews were delivered from the great danger that had been over them, and we read, "The Jews had light and gladness and joy and honor. And in every province and in every kingdom, wherever the king's command and his edict came, there was gladness and joy among the Jews, a feast and a holiday. And many from the peoples of the country became Jews, for the fear of the Jews had fallen upon them" (Esther 8:16, 17).

Ready Access Provided

These examples suffice to show that Gentiles had to become Jews in order to be saved before the time of Christ. With the coming of the Savior, everything was changed. God did not nullify His promises to Israel as a nation, but He did change the scope of salvation, removing all of the national and ceremonial barriers so that the Gentiles might have ready access to Him. The long rebellion of the people finally brought a terrible fruitage of judgment. At the very moment Christ died, there was an earthquake. The middle wall of partition which kept the Gentiles away from the temple area was broken down (Eph. 2:14). The veil in the Temple which had barred all but the great high priest was torn in two from top to bottom. By this God signified that He was utterly through with the Temple and with buildings, through with the sacrifices and the priesthood. Now, the one way to God was through the Lord Jesus Christ.

Israel was not cast away, but set aside, and through this fall salvation came to the Gentiles. We are the ones who can come boldly to God today, through the new and living way that has been prepared for us by the grace of God through the death and resurrection of our Lord Jesus Christ. He is the door (John 10:9). He is the way, the truth and the life (John 14:6). Now the human road of salvation is reversed. Instead of a Gentile being forced to come to God by changing his nationality, it is now necessary for a member of the ancient race to abandon his position and to accept the sinner's Savior.

Provoking Israel to Jealousy

One of the purposes that God had in this shift of method was that the people whom He chose in Abraham might be stimulated by a sort of jealousy to see the folly of their ways and to return to the Lord. Alas! There is little in Gentile Christendom today which could provoke Israel to jealousy. Rather we see that Gentiledom has gone back to the weak and beggarly elements of the law—that law which Christ died to free us from. We see today a form of religion which pours out huge sums to build great buildings called "sanctuaries." It is impossible to find anything like this in the New Testament. God does not live in a building. He lives in our day only in the hearts of those who have been born again. Our responsibility is very great. We must understand that it is our duty so to live, with our lights shining before men, that they may see the good works which develop in us from the presence of the indwelling Christ and glorify our Father which is in Heaven (Matt. 5:16). There is little in present-day Christendom which could arouse jealousy in Israel or in anyone else. Here and there we find those whose lives are springs flowing for Christ; wherever such people go there is refreshment for others of God's people and there is attraction toward Christ.

All of this is through the grace of God. What riches have now been made available for the whole world! God has now reconciled to Himself that which

Israel's Future Glory

He once cursed. "For God was in Christ reconciling the world to himself, not counting their trespasses against them, and entrusting to us the message of reconciliation" (2 Cor. 5:19).

RICHES FOR THE GENTILES

What riches have now been made available for the Gentiles! The word that the Jews used to identify the nations that had not been chosen in Abraham had become a terrible one to them. It is today to those of Israel who do not know Jesus Christ. The *goyim* were the nations that did not know Jehovah. Any contact with them brought uncleanness to Israel. Since Christ, the temporary setting aside of Israel has brought riches to us, the Gentiles. Now every man can come to the true God through the simple way that has been opened through Christ. Now the self-righteous philosopher if he will abandon his self-righteousness can come to God and find mercy, pardon and divine righteousness, made available through the Savior. Now the barbarous savage can be received by the God of all holiness if he will confess his sin and acknowledge that Jesus is the sin-bearer.

In the setting aside of Israel, God stepped out of the bounds of a national deity, bounds which He had imposed upon Himself, and became available to the whole of the human race. The Samaritan woman heard the prophecy of this change from the lips of Jesus Christ Himself. She had sought to change the subject when her utter sinfulness was revealed by His penetrating questions and analysis of her condition. She had said, "Sir, I perceive that you are a prophet. Our fathers worshipped on this mountain, and you say that Jerusalem is the place where men ought to worship" (John 4:20). The Lord did not sidestep the question, and He did not answer it in the way that many modern theologians would like to have had the question answered. Jesus clearly recognized the national limits of salvation which existed in His day and the geographical isolation of God's blessing at that time. Some would have liked to have had Him say that all religions are good, and that God can be approached in any way, any time and any place that man desires. This simply was not true then, nor is it true now.

The Lord Jesus announced the great change that was to come. God was going to burst the bounds that He had drawn around Himself in Israel and was going to bring riches to the world and the Gentiles. Jesus said, "Woman, believe me, the hour is coming when neither on this mountain nor in Jerusalem will you worship the Father. You worship what you do not know; we [Jews] worship what we know, for salvation is from the Jews. But the hour is coming, and now is, when the true worshippers will worship the Father in spirit and truth, for such the Father seeks to worship him" (John 4:21–23).

The Holy Spirit teaches us in the epistle to the Ephesians that before Christ came into the world all non-Jews were godless, hopeless and Christless (Eph. 2:11). Then God acted in judgment and set aside His ancient people, temporarily, in order that salvation might be brought to the Gentiles. Our text now gives us what might be called a mathematical inversion. If the setting aside of God's ancient people brought to us, Gentiles, the inestimable and incalculable blessings that we know in Christ; what will the restoration of this people be but life from the dead!

Unfulfilled Promises

The first teaching of our passage is that God intends to restore the Jews to the place of their former blessing. He is going to do it in His way and not in theirs. Beyond any valid question, the Bible teaches that God intends to keep His promises to Israel. Let us see what these unfulfilled promises are. I am not going to make mention of the promises which have already been fulfilled but only of those promises which have not been fulfilled. In the Lord Jesus Christ, Son of God and also Son of Abraham, blessings were made available for all the families of the earth (Gen. 12:3), but the national blessings have not yet been fulfilled.

The Lord made a covenant with Abraham that he and his seed would possess a great portion of what we call the Near East. It was a covenant that was confirmed by God's one-sided oath. He did not have Abraham swear because man's word is worthless even when he takes an oath. Thus God alone made the figure eight, circling the divided portions of the blood sacrifice in the ancient manner of confirming an oath. (Gen. 15:17). "In the same day the Lord made a covenant with Abram, saying, "Unto thy seed have I given this land, from the river of Egypt unto the great river, the river Euphrates: the Kenites, and the Kenizites, and the Kadmonites, and the Hittites, and the Perizzites and the Rephaims, and the Amorites, and the Canaanites, and the Girgashites, and the Jebusites" (Gen. 15:18–21).

Some of these landmarks have been lost to us, but those that we know are certain beyond doubt. Today the nation of Israel is little more than a beachhead on the Mediterranean in comparison with that which has been guaranteed to them by the Word of God. Before describing the limits of the lands which God has promised to Israel, it is necessary to say that if the present nation of Israel were destroyed and the Arab peoples were to push every Jew into the sea, it would not nullify the promises of God or make them of no effect. God has sworn by Himself and the promises will be fulfilled. Abraham's seed shall possess the land.

The Hittites

The land that is outlined in Genesis borders on the river of Egypt, which is a stream south of the Negeb, well south of Gaza, including territory that is at present in the hands of the Egyptians. It has been promised by God to Israel. The second border is "the great river, the river Euphrates." This means that the promised land includes the entire nation that is presently known as the Hashemite kingdom of Jordan as well as a portion of what is today known as Iraq. The amazing part of the promise is in the remainder of the verses. These verses describe territories that were once occupied by ten ancient nations. Until our generation the borders of these nations were unknown; several of them may not be known at present. One of them has become so well known in the last generation that there can be no doubt whatsoever. God has promised Israel that she shall possess the country formerly occupied by the Hittites.

A New Standard

It is also well-known that God told Moses that there would come a prophet like unto him (Deut. 18:15–19). It may well be that this prophecy will find its ultimate fulfillment when the witness of the tribulation period shall stand between God and the people to administer judgment and blessing.

It should also be recognized that God has announced in many places in the Old Testament that the marvelous things He will do on behalf of the Jews at the time of their restoration will be so beyond anything He has ever done in this earth that they will become a new standard by which power and wonder shall be measured.

At the same moment God gave Moses the tables of the law for the second time, God said, "Behold, I make a covenant. Before all your people I will do marvels, such as have not been wrought in all the earth or in any nation; and all the people among whom you are shall see the work of the Lord; for it is a terrible thing that I will do with you" (Exod. 34:10). It should be noted that in all the Jewish translations the last clause has been toned down to say less than the Hebrew really says. The work that God announces is not merely tremendous, but it is a tremendous or terrible work that the Lord is going to do with or by means of the Jews.

CHAPTER XIV

We have the story of some of the marvelous works which took place in the wilderness during the years of their wanderings. We remember the passage of the Jordan, the fall of Jericho, the wonders that were accomplished through the Judges—Gideon, Samson and the rest. But God announced through the later prophets that He would do works so much more wonderful that no one would even talk about the miracles done during the earlier history of Israel.

Listen to Micah. He tells of the blessings that are to come upon the people when they are restored and says, "According to the days of thy coming out of the land of Egypt will I show unto him marvelous things" (Mic. 7:15). On this verse Rabbi S. Goldman, in the famed Soncino edition of the Bible, says, "The exodus, throughout the Bible, is quoted as the example *par excellence* of divine intervention on Israel's behalf." Jeremiah announces the overturning of this standard of comparison. In the sixteenth chapter by the weeping prophet, we have the announcement of this amazing reversal.

Jewish Dispersion

God begins by describing the present centuries of Jewish dispersion throughout the world. If we are to understand the glories of the Jewish restoration, we must see the sad story that precedes it. First, God announces the terrible judgments that were to come upon the people and the land of Israel. These judgments have been fulfilled to the letter. The Lord then warns Jeremiah that the people will ask why these judgments have come upon them and the land, and gives Jeremiah the answer. "And it shall come to pass, when thou shalt tell this people all these words, and they shall say unto thee, Wherefore hath the Lord pronounced all this great evil against us? What is our iniquity? What is our sin that we have committed against the Lord our God? Then shaft thou say unto them, Because your fathers have forsaken me, saith the Lord, and have walked after other gods, and have served them. and have worshipped them, and have forsaken me, and have not kept my law; and ye have done worse than your fathers; for, behold, ye walk every one after the stubbornness of his evil heart, so that ye hearken not unto me; therefore will I cast you out of this land into a land that ye have not known, neither ye nor your fathers; and there shall ye serve other gods day and night; forasmuch as I will show you no favor" (Jer. 16:10–13). Those lands are surely Russia, Germany, the United States, and the other lands to which God has scattered His people. If all that was prophesied in judgment in the days of Jeremiah has come true in such detail, why shall we not believe all the more that the great promises of restoration shall also come true. The whole tone of the narrative changes and

Israel's Future Glory

the voice of promise is now heard: "Therefore, behold, the days come, saith the Lord, that it shall no more be said: As the Lord liveth, that brought up the children of Israel from the land of Egypt, but: As the Lord liveth, that brought up the children of Israel from the land of the north, and from all the countries whither he had driven them; and I will bring them back into their land that I gave unto their fathers. Behold, I will send for many fishers, saith the Lord, and they shall fish them; and afterward I will send for many hunters, and they shall hunt them from every mountain, and from every hill, and out of the clefts of the rocks. For mine eyes are upon all their ways, they are not hid from my face; neither is their iniquity concealed from mine eyes. And first I will recompense their iniquity and their sin double, because they have profaned my land . . ." (Jer. 16:14–18).

Restoration to the Land

Here is the outline of all that is to happen when God brings His people back into the land. He is going to give them the whole land and all that He has promised unto them. He will send Moses and Elijah to preach salvation and deliverance unto them. It is necessary that we underline Jeremiah's sentence, "At first I will recompense their iniquity and their sin double," for the time of Jacob's greatest trouble lies in those terrible months that have been limited by Daniel and by our Lord Jesus. Daniel told of the rise of the Antichrist, the restoration of the Jews, and of the troubles that should come upon them until Messiah should come out of Heaven to complete their deliverance. Jesus Christ Himself said, "For then there will be great tribulation, such as has not been from the beginning of the world until now, no, and never will be. And except those days should be shortened, no human being would be saved; but for the sake of the elect those days will be shortened" (Matt. 24:21, 22). The Lord spoke of this when He said, "He who endures to the end [of this period of tribulation] shall be saved [from the persecutions that shall be brought to an end.]"

Out of this preaching of Moses and Elijah comes the company of the 144,000 mentioned in the book of Revelation, composed of 12,000 men from each of the twelve tribes of Israel. These 144,000 are not any company living today. Do not be deceived by the preaching of the cults which announce that they are this particular group. The 144,000 cannot arise until Moses and Elijah have come to do their preaching, and these cannot come until the Lord Jesus has taken His church out before the beginning of the great tribulation.

The 144,000 are Jews. If any Jew should ask how the identity of the tribes shall be ascertained, when no Jew living today knows for sure to which of the tribes he belongs, I would remind him that when the eleven brothers came down into

Egypt at the time of Joseph, they did not know him, but he knew them. They were astonished when he directed them to their places at the table, each according to his rank and age among the brethren. So shall it be when the greater Joseph, the Lord Jesus Christ, intervenes on behalf of the Jews. He knows them, and will know them. When this 144,000 has been chosen, they will go out over the whole world like so many St. Paul's, or to be more correct, like 144,000 Jonahs who have been swallowed by the Gentile whale for these last three days and nights—these last three thousand years—and spit out into the holy land. Like Jonah they will be transformed, obedient and preaching the gospel of grace through Christ who will then be the Messiah of Israel. As we shall see, this will be for the whole of the earth, "life from the dead."

XV

Broken Branches

For if the dough offered as firstfruits is holy, the whole lump is also holy; and if the root is holy, so are the branches. But if some of the branches were broken off, and you, a wild olive shoot, were grafted in their place to share with them the root and fatness of the olive tree, do not boast over the branches. But if you do boast, remember that it is not you that support the root, but that the root supports you (Rom. 11:16–18).

The Jews Set Aside

So far in the eleventh chapter, the Holy Spirit has already shown us that God has not rejected His people, but that they are merely set aside temporarily. We have also seen that the elect nation of Israel was divided into two groups spiritually—those who were chosen by grace to remain faithful to the covenant of promise and those who hardened their hearts and were, consequently, brought by God to a condition of stupor so that their very blessings became a snare and a trap for them. This did not mean, even though a great majority fell away from God, that He had canceled His promises. In fact, the setting aside of the majority and the suspension of the national promises made it possible for God to turn to all the Gentile peoples of the world and offer free and gracious salvation to them. Thus it is evident that the temporary suspension has brought immeasurable blessing to innumerable multitudes. We are then told that the end of Israel's suspension and their ultimate restoration to the place of national blessing and privilege will be for the whole world a blessing so stupendous that it may be called "life from the dead."

CHAPTER XV

It is from this point that the Holy Spirit continues His argument by a double analogy drawn from two passages in the Old Testament. We read, "For if the small piece of dough offered as firstfruits is holy, the whole dough-mass is also holy; and if the root is holy, so are the branches."

Any Jew who heard this statement would immediately remember a paragraph that was given to Moses by God in the ceremonial law of the Pentateuch. In the book of Numbers we read (I take this quotation from the Jewish version according to the Masoretic text), "And the Lord spoke unto Moses, saying: Speak unto the children of Israel, and say unto them: When ye come into the land whither I bring you, then it shall be, that, when ye eat of the bread of the land, ye shall set apart for a gift unto the Lord. Of the first of your dough ye shall set apart a cake for a gift; as that which is set apart of the threshing-floor, so shall ye set it apart. Of the first of your dough ye shall give unto the Lord a portion for a gift throughout your generations" (Num. 15:17–21).*

This practice was so common among Jews that they would have understood perfectly what the writer was talking about. Both the part and the whole had to be considered as possessing the quality of holiness.

In order to understand this we must first realize that throughout the Old Testament the word "holy" has a special meaning. In the Old Testament "holy" means "separated from profane uses, consecrated to God." In the use of the allusion as found in our text, Paul is saying that if the whole nation of Israel was originally set apart for God by the call of Abraham and the giving of the covenant promises to him, then the individuals of the race of Abraham also have a special relationship to God. This does not mean that they are personally holy, for some of them are even accursed; but it does mean that the members of the ancient race have been chosen by God and they will be brought to fulfill His purposes.

Root and branches

The paragraphs that we now study have been one of the greatest fields for controversy in all of Biblical interpretation. I have before me at least a half dozen different interpretations of the parable of the olive tree which is about to be set forth by Paul in the course of his discussion. I believe that much of the difficulty

---

* *The Holy Scriptures* (1917 Translation), used by permission of The Jewish Publication Society, Philadelphia, Pa.

can be circumvented if we will understand one basic principle. This passage is not talking about individuals but is talking about Israel nationally, and the Gentiles collectively, in their relationships to God and the covenants of salvation.

The analogy is now repeated and made stronger by the comparison of the root of a tree with its branches. Since these two illustrations are parallel, we must see that the root is the whole of the nation as originally set apart by God in Abraham and that the branches are those that grow from him.

There has been much confusion among commentators through their failure to see that the branches in verse sixteen include all of the natural posterity of Abraham, whether of the apostate majority or of the believing minority. Only later will we consider the branches that are broken off the trunk and replaced by graftings from another tree. In the text as we are studying it, we must see that the root is Abraham and the tree is the whole line of the patriarchs and people of Israel. Whether individuals were good or evil, they still were the transmitters of the promises and covenant which God had given to Abraham.

A few years ago, a New York clergyman wrote a doctoral thesis on *The Meaning of the Olive Tree in Romans XI*. From this thesis I take the basis for the above conclusion, while differing from the author, Dr. Myles Bourke, in the application. He says, "Evidently, *agia* (holy) in this passage cannot denote an actual internal state of acceptability to God; while that notion could apply to the root (Abraham), it could hardly be transferred to the branches without distinction; it could not apply to those which had been cut off the tree, and it is those which the apostle had foremost in mind. Saint Paul argues from an actual situation, not a possible one; the conversion of the Jews is possible and to be expected because of a quality which even in their state of infidelity they possess; the quality, namely, of holiness, consecration to God, implied in belonging to the race which was set apart to God in its first members and founders. This is the basis of the apostle's hope. The entire race has been consecrated to God, and this consecration must then extend to all its members, even those whose dispositions make them unworthy members of it. But if the unbelieving Jews are consecrated to God, then there is every reason to believe that God will bring them to a state in which their interior dispositions will correspond to the dignity which they possess now only as an external quality."

I am afraid that Dr. Bourke looks upon this hope of conversion as something that might take place in our time. That this is not so is firmly stated later in our chapter (vs. 25, 26). He would have saved himself great labor if, instead of arguing his case, he had been willing to quote a paragraph or two from John Calvin and a footnote from the editor of Calvin's English translation.

CHAPTER XV

Jews vs. Gentiles

The great Reformer wrote on this passage, "By comparing the worthiness of the Jews and of the Gentiles, Paul now takes away pride from the one and pacifies the other, as far as he can, for he shows that the Gentiles, if they pretended to any honor of their own, did in no respect excel the Jews; in fact, that if they came to a contest, the Gentiles would be left far behind. Let us remember that in this comparison man is not compared with man, but nation with nation. If then a comparison be made between them, they shall be found equal in this respect, that they are both equally the children of Adam; the only difference is that the Jews had been separated from the Gentiles so that they might be a special people for the Lord." Calvin continues to say that they were then sanctified by the holy covenant (made with Abraham) and given special honors that God did not then give to the Gentiles. At the time Paul was writing, the power of the covenant seemed a very small thing. Therefore, Paul bids us look back to Abraham and the patriarchs in whom the blessing of God was neither empty nor void. Paul concludes that a hereditary holiness had passed to all their posterity. This conclusion would have been impossible if he had been speaking of individual persons and it would have been impossible if he had not remembered the unchangeableness of the promise of God. When a father is good, he cannot transmit his goodness to his son. But when the Lord chose Abraham and set him apart for a special purpose, that his seed might also be holy; God conferred a special holiness—we might better say an apartness—not only on Abraham personally, but also on his whole race.

John Owen, the translator and editor of Calvin's *Romans*, makes this truth doubly clear in his note. He writes, "That the holiness here mentioned is external and relative, not personal and inward, is evident from the whole context. The children of Israel were called holy in all their wickedness and disobedience because they had been consecrated to God, adopted as His people, and set apart for His service, and they enjoyed all the external privileges of the covenant which God had made with their fathers." He then quotes an ancient writer, Pareus, who describes just what qualities can be transmitted from father to offspring and what cannot be thus transmitted. "Often," he says, "the worst descend from the best and the best from the worst; from wicked Ahaz sprang good Hezekiah; from Hezekiah descended impious Manassa; from Manassa came good Josiah; and from Josiah sprang wicked sons, Shallum and Jehoiakim." Owen then comments, "But all were alike holy in the sense intended here by the apostle, as they were circumcised and had inherited the transmissible rights and privileges of the covenant."

Broken Branches

Another commentator, Walter Scott, writes: "The attentive reader will readily perceive that *relative* holiness, or consecration to God, is here exclusively meant ... Abraham was as it were the root of the visible [Israel]. Ishmael was broken off and the tree grew up in Isaac; and when Esau was broken off, it grew up in Jacob and his sons. When the nation rejected the Messiah, their relation to Abraham and to God was, as it were, suspended. They no longer retained even the outward seal of the covenant, for circumcision then lost its validity and baptism became the [outward] sign of regeneration; they were [as a nation] from that time forward deprived of the ordinances of God."

Promises without Condition

We sum up as follows: The whole world fell into sin in Adam and all men died spiritually in that disobedience. In the fullness of time, God proceeded with His plan and chose Abraham. It is well to remember the great explanation of this choice as recorded in Isaiah's prophecy; "Hearken to me, ye that follow after righteousness, ye that seek the Lord; Look unto the rock whence ye were hewn, and to the hole of the pit whence ye were digged. Look unto Abraham your father, and unto Sarah that bore you; for when he was but one I called him, and I blessed him, and made him many" (Isa. 51:1, 2). The many that came out of Abraham are set apart for God. The fact that the majority of them rebelled against God cannot change the promises of God; there is no withdrawal of an unconditional promise, and the promises to Abraham were made without condition. We must understand, therefore, that even though many of the children of Abraham have gone into great evil, they are carrying on the physical process of begetting children who are of this separate nation. In the fulness of time, God is going to do something with that people. If their present suspension has brought blessing to the whole world of believers—Jew and Gentile alike—what will their national regathering be but life from the dead?

The apostle continues with the argument. Some of the natural branches of the covenant tree were broken off. In their place God has grafted shoots of a wild olive tree.

Grafting

Grafting is one of the most interesting phases of gardening and horticulture. Many plants are almost useless unless they are grafted to a rootstock that is different

CHAPTER XV

from their own. The best roses are grafted to strong roots which, if left to themselves, would not produce beautiful blooms. At the close of the last century, a great infestation practically destroyed all of the grape vines in France. The vineyards of France were saved only because strong roots of California vines that were immune to phylloxera were brought in and the scions of the famed French vines were grafted onto them. There is scarcely a grape vine in France today that is not growing on California roots.

Because of the existence of this figure of speech in the Bible, I have spent many hours studying the whole question of grafting. There is considerable literature on the subject, going back many centuries. Especially has there been discussion on the influence of the stock or root on the scion. The best authorities state simply that they do not have the answers to the problems involved. When a scion is grafted into a rootstock, the union is a growth from each. This double growth fuses into a mass so continuous that precise location of the line of union is frequently impossible even with the aid of a microscope. For this reason I am convinced that the symbol must be taken only in the broadest sense. There is no use in attempting to push the matter, because the entire Bible would teach us that all of the life of the individual must come from the Lord Jesus Christ. There is no life apart from Him.

Since there is no life apart from Christ, we must understand this entire metaphor in the light of what we have seen in the sixth chapter of this epistle. There we saw that Adam was considered as the federal head of the race in the first instance and that Christ was considered as the federal head of the race in the second instance. This means that God counted every descendant of Adam, the entire human race, as being in Adam and as having spiritually died in Adam's death; and that God counted every believer in Christ as having died and risen in the death and resurrection of Christ. God the Father made the unconditional covenant and promises to Abraham and Christ (Gal. 3:16). These promises were both national and individual. The individual promises have to do with the relationship of each individual soul with the Savior. The national promises have to do with God's overall dealing with the human race and the final consummation of His plan to triumph over all the forces of evil and bring righteousness to this earth. Abraham is the root of the olive tree and the branches are those that grow out of Abraham, whether nationally or individually. It is important to see this, lest one fall into the error of applying this only to the relationship of individual believers. There is yet a national fulfillment of these promises, and the failure to see this makes nonsense of many of the verses of this chapter.

Broken Branches

The Olive Tree

In the Old Testament there are two prophecies concerning the olive tree, both referring to Israel as a nation. The one describes the fair olive tree and the breaking off of some of its branches; the other prophecy describes the restoration of the branches and the ultimate glory of the olive tree. In Jeremiah we read, "The Lord called thy name. A leafy olive tree, fair with goodly fruit; with the noise of a great tumult He hath kindled fire upon it, and the branches of it are broken" (Jer. 11:16). This is the picture of Israel, nationally, today. But listen to Hosea tell of that which is yet future, "I will be as the dew unto Israel; he shall blossom as the lily and cast forth his roots as Lebanon. His branches shall spread, and his beauty shall be as the olive tree, and his fragrance as Lebanon. They that dwell under his shadow shall again make corn to grow and shall blossom as the vine; the scent thereof shall be as the vine of Lebanon. Ephraim [shall say] What have I to do any more with idols?" (Hos. 14:5–9).

Today we live in the day of the broken branches of Israel. Onto the root and stock of Abraham, God grafted the multitude of Gentile believers, but the Gentiles have come to presume upon the grace of God, just as Israel did in the days of her first great apostasy. The individual who knows that his blessings are through Jesus Christ, the son of Abraham, must ever remain humble. He must understand the plan of God, love the people of Israel, and pray for the peace of Jerusalem. The mass of Gentiles who have come into Christendom, though they are not within true Christianity, must not boast. With the coming of true Christianity to the Gentiles, a mixed multitude came under the shade of the olive tree. There was a grafting into the rich, leafy olive tree for the fulfillment of God's national purposes as well as for the fulfillment of His plan for the lives of some individuals.

The power of the Jews as a reigning, governing people was set aside and the times of the Gentiles began. Those times have run for almost three thousand years and Gentile nations still dominate the world scene. Gentile world forces were grafted onto the stock of Abraham in order to fulfill God's purposes in government. Individual Gentiles were grafted into the true olive tree to make up the body of Christ, the true church. Both of these works must be kept in mind as distinct from each other. Gentile America, for example, has the root and fatness of earthly promises that were made to Israel. This is God's doing and we must not boast about it. Other Gentile nations are also fulfilling God's governmental plans in the world at this time, but we must not forget that we are all to be broken off as nations sometime in the future. God is going to fulfill His purposes in Israel.

CHAPTER XV

Kipling saw much more deeply than he may have imagined when he wrote in his famed "Recessional,"

> Such boastings as the Gentiles use
>   Or lesser breeds without the law.

There is a distinct sense in which some Gentile nations have been blessed of God and grafted into the office of bearers of blessing to the world. Let them not boast. Especially let us, as nations, remember the importance of Israel in the world. It is not we who support the root, but the root supports us. The blessings we have today are blessings that God originally promised to Abraham, and one day God will give them back to Abraham's seed.

XVI

The Times of the Gentiles

You will say, Branches were broken off that I might be grafted in. That is true. They were broken off because of their unbelief, but you stand fast only through faith. So do not become proud, but stand in awe. For if God did not spare the natural branches, neither will he spare you. Note then the kindness and severity of God; severity toward those who have fallen; but God's kindness to you, provided you continue in his kindness; otherwise you too will be cut off.

They also, if they abide not still in unbelief, shall be grafted in: for God is able to graft them in again. For if you were cut out of the olive tree which is wild by nature and were grafted contrary to nature into a good olive tree: how much more shall these, which are the natural branches, be grafted into their own olive tree? (Rom. 11:19–24).

The entire human race stems from Adam, and in Adam all men died spiritually. In Abraham God started a new thing and chose a special people through grace in order that certain purposes might be fulfilled. These purposes are both national and individual. God promised Abraham that through him all the nations would be blessed and that through him all the families of the earth would be blessed. These two purposes are distinct and different.

In the eleventh chapter of Romans we have seen important teachings from God concerning these varied purposes. The truth centers in a metaphor concerning a good olive tree from which certain branches were broken off, only to be replaced by branches from a wild olive tree. Abraham is the root and national Israel is the trunk of the tree. The majority of the individuals of Israel became apostate more than two thousand years ago and God broke off the branches, by taking away their land, their city, and their Temple. Gentile world powers, especially the

Roman Empire and the heirs of that empire in the western world, became the heirs of God's national promises.

The Tower of Babel

If we are to understand God's purposes among the nations, it will be necessary for us to go back to the beginning of nations and see the order that God announced at that time. The growth of nations was not a slow phenomenon but a catastrophic judgment. Nations and the differences between them were created by God after the tower of Babel, both as a curse upon mankind and as a step in working out the fixed purposes of God.

Before Babel the whole population of the world was of one language and of one speech. When Noah and his sons came out of the ark, the human race was limited to three families. All of the peoples of the earth stem from these three branches, the sons of Shem, Ham and Japheth. The interplay among these three racial groups has caused most of the wars of human history. An outline of the struggle between Shem, Ham and Japheth will reveal the past course of history. The prophecies of the Bible concerning them will reveal to us the direction in which history must move.

Modern historians, for the most part, have adopted an evolutionary attitude toward history. They see no interrelationship between events that transpired far from each other in time and space but whose true meaning demands a frame of reference which has been neglected or rejected by the writers of history. Human events are treated as purely human phenomena. Unwilling to believe that God has intervened in the affairs of men, that He continues to do so, and even more unwilling to believe that a personal devil is the prince of this world and the god of this age, they are often totally unable to see the spiritual and invisible causes above and beyond the earthly arena. They confuse Satan's puppets for God's real, live actors. Events which are really consequent they treat as unrelated; incidents which are truly inseparable they record as though the happenings took place on different planets.

A Curse and a Blessing

After the flood Noah became drunk and lay in his tent. His son, Ham, went into the tent and something horrible took place. Just what is hidden beneath the words of the Scripture account. We may remind ourselves that Sodom and Gomorrah are included within the bounds of the territory of Ham (Gen. 10:19). He came out and talked about to his brothers, Shem and Japheth, who took a garment and, backing into the tent, covered their father's nakedness. When Noah awoke, he knew what had taken place, and, undoubtedly under the inspiration of the Holy Spirit, pronounced a curse and a blessing on his sons, which have had more influence on subsequent human history than have almost any other lines spoken in history.

The curse which was pronounced by Noah was brief but very comprehensive. "Cursed be Canaan; a slave of slaves shall he be unto his brethren. And he said, Blessed be the Lord God of Shem; Canaan shall be his slave. God shall enlarge Japheth, and he shall dwell in the tents of Shem; Canaan shall be his slave" (Gen. 9:25–27).

Satan has attempted to obscure the history of the great defeat of the Hamitic peoples by circulating the slanderous lie that the Negro race is the sole descendent of Ham, and that their color and slavery are the result of the curse of Noah. We believe that the genealogical tables of the tenth chapter of Genesis refute this teaching. As far as we can ascertain, nobody in all history ever suggested that the Negroes were cursed from Ham before the middle of the last century. The idea was created out of whole cloth by those who wished for help in their unbiblical support of slavery.

The Bible and history unite to show that the Hamitic peoples were the Egyptians, the Canaanites, the Hittites, the Phoenecians and the Carthaginians. The great wars of the ancient world ultimately ended in the destruction of the power of Egypt, the Hittites, and finally of Rome's great enemy, Carthage. Only in our day has Egypt become once more a menace to Israel. This in itself is one more indication that the times of the Gentiles are drawing to a close.

Ham's Conflict with Israel

In choosing Abraham, God set forth that He intended to judge the world through the children of Shem. This is the national olive tree. Abraham was the chosen seed for government, and in him shall all the nations of the earth be blessed. The first great human wars were those in which Satan attempted to use the nations of Ham to destroy the nation of Abraham to which God had committed all government. It would seem that one of the grandsons of Ham took up the curse of God as a challenge and warred against God, against the divine judgment, and against the people who had been promised superiority over his family.

The history of the Jews records this fact in a striking manner. The great historian, Josephus, who lived about the time of Christ and wrote from a Jewish point of view, has the following to say about the sons of Ham and their conflict with Israel, "They, imagining the prosperity they enjoyed was not derived from the favor of God, but supposing that their own power was the proper cause of the plentiful condition they were in, did not obey him. Nay, they added to their disobedience of the divine will the suspicion that they were therefore ordered to send out separate colonies, that being divided asunder they might the more easily be oppressed. Now it was Nimrod who excited them to such an affront and contempt of God. He was the grandson of Ham the son of Noah, a bold man and of great strength of hand. He persuaded them not to ascribe it to God, as though it were through His means they were happy, but to believe that it was their own courage that procured that happiness. He also gradually changed the government into tyranny, seeing no other way of turning men from the fear of God but to bring them into a constant dependence upon his power. He also said he would be revenged on God, if He should have a mind to drown the world again and that he would avenge himself on God for destroying their forefathers.

"Now the multitude were very ready to follow the determination of Nimrod, and to esteem it a piece of cowardice to submit to God; they built a tower, neither sparing any pains, nor being in any degree negligent about the work; and, by reason of the multitude of hands employed on it, it grew very high, sooner than anyone could expect; but the thickness of it was so great, and it was so strongly built, that thereby its great height seemed, upon the view, to be less than it really was. It was built of burnt brick, cemented together with mortar, made of bitumen, that it might not be liable to admit water. When God saw that they acted so madly, He did not resolve to destroy them utterly, since they were not grown wiser by the destruction of the former sinners; but He caused a tumult among them, by producing in them divers languages; and causing that through the multitude of those languages, they should not be able to understand one another. The place wherein they built their tower is now called Babylon, for the Hebrews meant by the word Babel, 'Confusion.'"

Shem and Japheth

We pass over Josephus' effort to put all of the blame upon Nimrod and the Hamites. The sons of Shem and Japheth were in rebellion against God as much as were the sons of Ham. Although the entire race was involved in the rebellion at Babel and was included in the judgment of tongues and nations, the blessing of God did remain on the sons of Shem in a special way and on the sons of Japheth in a secondary way. It is that difference which is set forth in our text in the book of Romans. Government was established in Abraham and given to the sons of Shem. Japheth did succeed in destroying the power of Ham. What was to be the relationship between the sons of Japheth and the sons of Shem? The ancient prophecy announced a prior blessing for Shem, but a secondary blessing for Japheth. If we leave out the parts that apply to Ham, the verse reads as follows: "Blessed be the Lord God of Shem . . . God shall enlarge Japheth, and he shall dwell in the tents of Shem . . ." (Gen. 9:25–27).

In the epistle to the Romans, Paul is addressing Japheth. We might paraphrase our text to read: "Japheth will say, Jewish branches were broken off that I might be grafted in. That is true. They were broken off because of unbelief [and you came to dwell in their tents as God promised through Noah] but you stand fast only through faith. So do not become proud, but stand in awe. For if God did not spare the natural [Jewish] branches, neither will he spare you [Japheth]."

A National Matter

Incalculable harm has been done by those who have attempted to apply our text primarily to individuals. An individual who is once grafted into Christ by faith can never be broken off from Christ. He is not going to be a mutilated trunk in Heaven forever. It is theologically an error to think such a thing. When it is seen that Paul is speaking of the Jews' being removed, nationally, to be replaced nationally by Gentiles, we are fully prepared for that which will follow in a few verses.

It is certain that spiritual Israel had never been broken from the olive tree. Those who had believed before the time of Christ were in the place of blessing which God had planned for them and which He had given them by promise. The individual Jews like Paul, who had believed in the time of Paul were certainly a part of the spiritual olive tree. All of the root and fatness of the stock belonged to them and they were blessed with faithful Abraham.

All that had been broken off were the individuals who had remained in unbelief. These were the dominant characters in national Israel. They, by their mass unbelief, had caused God to bring upon the people the curses which He had announced at the time of the nation's youth. As a nation Israel was broken off from the national promises of God. It is as a nation that Israel will again be grafted into the olive tree and will become the people of God. Let us realize that this will not come in our day. While the true church is on earth, Israel will continue in blindness with a few individual exceptions until the time of our full redemption is come. Their unbelief will continue in ever-hardening enmity until the climax of their rebellion has come and the cup of wrath is filled to the full. It is not until the terrible moment that is called in the Old Testament "the time of Jacob's trouble" (Jer. 30:7) and in the New Testament by the Lord Jesus Christ himself, "the great tribulation" (Matt. 24:21), that Israel will come to the Messiah as a people. Our Lord told us that they would be in peril of the Gentiles until the end and that only when "they shall *see* the sign of the Son of Man in Heaven" (Matt. 24:30) will they have faith This sign will be the fulfillment of the prophecy in which God told Zechariah that "they shall look on me whom they have pierced" (Zech. 12:10).

Thomas a Picture of Israel

All of this is pictured by an incident that took place after the resurrection of our Lord Jesus Christ. Among the disciples was Thomas, who is called doubting Thomas to this day because of his unbelieving attitude toward the Lord Jesus and the life after death. Thomas was undoubtedly being true to his own mentality, but God was using him as a character actor to show forth the whole future of the Jewish nation. Thomas was absent at the time the Lord first appeared to the other disciples. When they told him about it, he said, "Except I shall see in his hands the print of the nails, and put my finger into the print of the nails, and thrust my hand into his side, I will not believe" (John 20:25). This is a plain picture of the life of Israel today. They will not believe, and it is futile to think of any mass conversion of the members of that race and religion. The time will come when the Lord Jesus shall appear in Heaven and Israel shall see Him as Zechariah promised. The Lord will be as gracious to the nation as a whole as He was to Thomas individually. If the Lord had rejected Thomas, it would have been no more than just; but when Christ came back to the disciples the next time, He began by inviting Thomas to touch him, to put his finger into the wound in the Lord's hand, and to thrust his hand into the side of the Savior. It is thus that the Lord will deal with all Israel in that future day. The unbelieving people will see Him and, in looking upon Him whom they have pierced, they will know Him and bow before Him. Their national conversion will not come until that day. So we must insist that we are to expect no spiritual mass movement among them in our time. We are to welcome the few who have come, not as members of Israel, but as members of Adam, *sinners*, members of the lost race who must take the Lord Jesus Christ as any sinner must take the Savior.

The Church Not a Temporal Power

Just as certain as it is that spiritual Israel has never been broken off from the olive tree, just so certain it is that the church has not been grafted into the position of Israel as a nation. One of the saddest things in all church history is the pretention that the church is to have temporal power. Neither Peter nor the disciples made any pretense of temporal power when they were here on earth. The Lord Jesus had announced that His kingdom was not of this world, and that is the reason why His servants did not fight (John 18:36). We cannot imagine that the Lord Jesus would live in a palace today and have uniformed guards with spears. How did it come about that a part of the church claimed to have temporal power? Whenever I read the history of the early dark ages, I am reminded of the dog in the fable by Aesop. You remember the story of the dog who crossed the bridge with a bone in his mouth and looked down into the water. He saw his reflection, bone and all, and fancied that it was another dog. He thought that the bone in the water was bigger and better than the bone in his own mouth and so he snapped at the dog in the water. Naturally his bone dropped into the water and he got nothing in its place.

This is a very good example of the church in the fourth, fifth, and sixth centuries. The Lord had given to the church great spiritual gifts. When the Roman Empire began to break up before the inroads of the Germanic tribes, the church saw the power of the emperors being dissipated. Thinking that earthly power was worth having, the church snapped at these powers of wealth and government and lost her spiritual power in that moment. From then on there was little spiritual power in Christendom until Luther and Calvin returned to the Word of God as the source of their power and God began to bless them again in His wonderful grace.

Gentile Power

The church as a governmental whole is certainly not in the mind of God when Paul speaks of branches of the wild olive being grafted into the natural olive tree. The secular Gentile powers, (the Roman Empire and its successors, especially) are those branches. The breaking off of the Jewish branches had begun long before the time of Christ. Israel had begun her history as a slave people in Egypt. They should have remembered the taste of this miserable dust, but they soon forgot God when they came into the land flowing with milk and honey. Their early history in Palestine tells of a series of captivities as they were brought to toil under the neighboring Philistines whom God would have destroyed had His people remained faithful to Him. Time after time He raised the judges—Gideon, Samson and the rest—to redeem His people.

There was a long period of liberty and even glory under David and Solomon, but the sin of the people soon brought on the great captivity in which they were forced into Babylon, to sing the songs of Zion in a strange land (Ps. 137). They were not back from Babylon very long before the armies of Alexander the Great moved in upon them. These were followed by the powers of Alexander's generals, and then the Romans moved in The armies of Rome were there in the days of the Lord and remained there until the forces of Islam took over. Israel has not been free until recent years. The beachhead that she holds in Palestine today is not to be taken for the fulfillment of the promises of God.

What we have described—Babylon, Greece, Rome—all this together is the power of the Gentiles. This is the Gentile domination that we must see as being the wild olive branches grafted into the place of the true branches.

We must look much more deeply at the warning which concludes our text. The kindness and the severity of God is seen in His dealings with the nations. God has been very severe toward Israel in the fall of Jerusalem, the wanderings among the nations, the Inquisition, the pogroms of Poland, the horrors of Hitler's prison camps, and communistic anti-semitism. God's severity toward Israel is not quite over. God has been very gracious toward the Gentile nations. His greatest grace has been reserved for the United States in our generation. Never has any people been so blessed, and never have so many sinned against so much grace. On the whole we do not want God's way, even though we talk about religion a great deal and have "God" in much of our conversation. Yet the word stands written; the Gentile nations, including ourselves, shall be cut off.

XVII

Israel's Deliverance

For I would not, brethren, that ye should be ignorant of this mystery, lest ye should be wise in your own conceits; that blindness in part is happened to Israel, until the fulness of the Gentiles be come in. And so all Israel shall be saved: as it is written, There shall come out of Sion the Deliverer, and shall turn away ungodliness from Jacob: For this is my covenant unto them, when I shall take away their sins. As concerning the gospel, they are enemies for your sakes: but as touching the election, they are beloved for the father's sake. For the gifts and calling of God are without repentance. (Rom. 11:25–29).

At last Paul is able to write the message his heart has longed to declare. God is going to restore Israel. Paul yearned for the salvation of his people. "Brethren, my heart's desire and prayer to God for Israel is, that they might be saved. For I bear them record that they have a zeal of God, but not according to knowledge. For they being ignorant of God's righteousness, and going about to establish their own righteousness, have not submitted themselves unto the righteousness of God. For Christ is the end of the law for righteousness to every one that believeth" (Rom. 10:1–4).

Salvation for Israel

Paul's desire for his people's salvation was not a vain wish. Had it been possible, the apostle would have been willing to be cursed by God if it could have brought about the salvation of his brethren. "I say the truth in Christ; I lie not, my conscience also bearing me witness in the Holy Ghost, That I have great heaviness and continual sorrow in my heart. For I could wish that myself were accursed from Christ for my brethren, my kinsmen according to the flesh: Who are Israelites; to whom pertaineth the adoption, and the glory, and the covenants, and the giving of the law, and the service of God, and the promises; Whose are the fathers, and of whom as concerning the flesh Christ came, who is over all, God blessed for ever. Amen" (Rom. 9:1–5).

We have seen in our study of the ninth chapter of the epistle how the great apostle defends his brethren after the flesh. He points out how this ancient people were the objects of God's grace and mercy (9:6–18). Israel was also the object of God's sovereignty and integrity (9:19–29). Their great stumbling block was Christ (9:30–33).

Though Israel did fall into unbelief as a nation, Paul hastens to remind us that there is personal salvation for each individual Jew. As individuals, they still are the objects of God's grace. They are to have faith in Christ as Savior (10:4–13). They are to give heed to the gospel (10:14–17). The offer of salvation to Israel is due to God's sovereign grace (10:18–21).

The apostle does not allow the Gentiles to forget that Israel's fall has made possible their blessing (Rom. 11:7–12). Gentiles are to remember that there is a remnant according to the election of grace to be found among God's ancient people (11:1–6). Furthermore, Paul argues, if through Israel's fall the blessing of salvation has been brought to the Gentile world, what greater blessing must await the world through Israel's ultimate restoration (11:13–24)?

Having presented Israel's case, Paul is ready to make the declaration for which he has long waited, "And so all Israel shall be saved!" The original text allows us to say, "and all Israel shall be delivered." This is a better translation, for as the context indicates, Israel's deliverance will be not only spiritual but political as well.

The passage of this study raises three questions: When is the time of this deliverance? What is the nature of this deliverance? What is the basis for such a deliverance? To these questions Paul now gives his attention.

Time of Deliverance

There can be no doubt of the fact that Israel is in a state of spiritual blindness. This is due to their hardness of heart against God and His Messiah. Isaiah graphically describes their sad condition: "Therefore is judgment far from us, neither doth justice overtake us; we wait for light, but behold obscurity; for brightness, but we walk in darkness. We grope for the wall like the blind, and we grope as if we had no eyes; we stumble at noon day as in the night; we are in desolate places as dead men. We roar all like bears, and mourn sore like doves; we look for judgment, but there is none; for salvation, but it is far off from us. For our transgressions are multiplied before thee, and our sins testify against us; and as for our iniquities, we know them. In transgressing and lying against the Lord and departing away from our God, speaking oppression and revolt, conceiving and uttering from the heart words of falsehood. And judgment is turned away backward, and justice standeth afar off; for truth is fallen in the street, and equity cannot enter" (Isa. 59:9–14). As we have seen in a previous study, this condition is the result of a judicial pronouncement which God made against His people. God Himself confirmed this judicial pronouncement to Isaiah, "And he said, Go, and tell this people, Hear ye indeed, but understand not; and see ye indeed, but perceive not. Make the heart of this people fat, and make their ears heavy, and shut their eyes; lest they see with their eyes, and hear with their ears, and understand with their heart, and convert, and be healed. Then said I, Lord, how long? And he answered, Until the cities be wasted without inhabitant, and the houses without man, and the land be utterly desolate. And the Lord have removed men far away, and there be a great forsaking in the midst of the land" (Isa. 6:9–12).

But this tragic state of affairs in which Israel finds herself will not last forever. "Blindness in part is happened to Israel, until the fulness of the Geniles be come in." Now, God is working out man's spiritual destiny through the redeemed of the Lord Jesus Christ. Man's historical destiny is being worked out through the Gentile nations. The times of "the fulness of the Gentiles" is described in Daniel, chapter 11. "And the king shall do according to his will; and he shall exalt himself, and magnify himself above every god, and shall speak marvellous things against the God of gods, and shall prosper till the indignation be accomplished: for that which is determined shall be done. Neither shall he regard the God of his fathers, nor the desire of women, nor regard any god; for he shall magnify himself above all. But in his estate shall he honor the God of forces: and a god whom his fathers knew not shall he honor with gold, and silver, and with precious stones, and pleasant things. Thus shall he do in the strong holds with a strange god, whom he shall acknowledge and increase with glory: and he shall cause them to rule over many, and shall divide the land for gain. And at the time of the end shall the king of the south push at him; and the king of the north shall come against him like a whirlwind, with chariots, and with horsemen, and with many ships; and he shall enter into the countries, and shall overflow and pass over. He shall enter also into the glorious land, and many countries shall be overthrown: but these shall escape out of his hand, even Edom, and Moab, and the chief of the children of Ammon. He shall stretch forth his hand also upon the countries: and the land of Egypt shall not escape. But he shall have power over the treasures of gold and of silver, and over all the precious things of Egypt: and the Libyans and the Ethiopians shall be at his steps. But tidings out of the east and out of the north shall trouble him: therefore he shall go forth with great fury to destroy, and utterly to make away many. And he shall plant the tabernacles of his palace between the seas in the glorious holy mountain; yet he shall come to his end, and none shall help him" (Dan. 11:36–45).

In the preceding verses, the prophet has traced the course of Gentile history as it will affect Israel and the Holy Land. The climax of this history will manifest itself in an unparalleled hatred of God and an attempt by an ungodly alliance to destroy Him and His people. The Gentiles will know God's judgment; Israel will know God's deliverance.

Paul now tells us how the deliverance of Israel is possible. "And so all Israel shall be saved; as it is written, There shall come out of Sion the Deliverer, and shall turn away ungodliness from Jacob; For this is my covenant unto them, when I shall take away their sins" (Rom. 11:26, 27). The Messiah will come, the Deliverer for whom Israel waits. No longer will He be the meek and lowly Lamb; He will be the roaring, raging Lion of the Tribe of Judah. As He judges the Gentiles, He will turn ungodliness from Jacob.

The New Covenant

How will this be accomplished? God Himself will do it through a new covenant which He will make with Israel when He takes away their sins. This new covenant is to be made with Israel and Judah and, therefore, is not to be confused with the covenant of grace which God already has made with the Church. This new covenant will be unconditional, and thus will not be dependent upon Israel's obedience. This covenant is described by the Prophet Jeremiah: "Behold, the days come, saith the Lord, that I will make a new covenant with the house of Israel, and with the house of Judah; Not according to the covenant that I made with their fathers in that day that I took them by the hand to bring them out of the land of Egypt; which my covenant they brake, although I was an husband unto them, saith the Lord" (Jer. 31:31, 32). Here, God contrasts His two covenants with Israel. The first covenant was conditional; its success depended upon Israel's faithfulness and obedience. "Now therefore, if ye will obey my voice indeed and keep my covenant, then ye shall be a peculiar treasure unto me above all people; for all the earth is mine. And ye shall be unto me a kingdom of priests, and an holy nation. These are the words which thou shalt speak unto the children of Israel" (Exod. 19:5, 6). The second covenant which God is to make with Israel is unconditional and its success is dependent upon God's sovereign elective grace alone. "But this shall be the covenant that I will make with the house of Israel; After those days, saith the Lord, I will put my law in their inward parts, and write it in their hearts; and will be their God, and they shall be my people" (Jer. 31:33). The first covenant set forth before Israel what was pleasing to God. It made great demands upon the people. However, though it made provisions for a broken law, the first covenant could never empower one with the ability to obey it. By contrast, the second covenant is to make new men of Israel. A nation will be born in a day. God will put His law into their inward parts and write it in their hearts. He will be their God and they shall be His people. God will manifest His sovereign electing grace on a national scale in behalf of Israel, even as He showed His sovereign elective grace on a personal scale to those who believed in Christ Jesus as Savior and Lord.

We do not need to confuse the new covenant which God is to make with Israel with the covenant of grace which God has made with believers in the Lord Jesus Christ. In the first instance, the new one is addressed to the house of Israel and Judah. In the second place, it is to take the place of the previous covenant which God has made with Israel through Moses. In the third place, it is to be made with the house of Israel "after those days," which is to say, "after the fulness of the Gentiles has come in." In the fourth place, God will transform the house of Israel by putting His law into their inward parts and writing it on their hearts. At this point, we might observe that this has not happened to us, even as believers in the Lord Jesus Christ. To be sure, we have been made new creatures in Christ Jesus, but we must still grow in grace and in the knowledge of the Lord Jesus Christ. We must be taught by the Holy Spirit and by the Word of God. The reason we study the Word of God is simply because it does not yet dwell within our hearts as it will dwell in the hearts of restored Israel.

In the fifth place, Israel will know the Lord, from the least to the greatest of them. This will not be any attainment of theirs, but it will be the result of a sovereign act of divine grace. "And they shall teach no more every man his neighbor, and every man his brother, saying, know the Lord; for they shall all know me, from the least of them unto the greatest of them, saith the Lord; for I will forgive their iniquity, and I will remember their sin no more" (Jer. 31:34). This new covenant which God will make with Israel differs from the Church's covenant of grace in that Israel will never depart from the Lord again. "And they shall be my people, and I will be their God; And I will give them one heart, and one way, that they may fear me for ever, for the good of them and of their children after them; And I will make an everlasting covenant with them, that I will not turn away from them, to do them good; but I will put my fear in their hearts, that they shall not depart from me" (Jer. 32:38–40). In sadness we must confess that this is not true of the covenant of grace. To be sure, once we come to the saving knowledge of the Lord Jesus Christ, we are eternally saved by sovereign grace. But how many of us become bad saints, disobedient children of God, as we refuse to walk in the light of God's Word? The Holy Spirit convicts us of sin and gives us no peace until we make a full surrender to the will of God. When God restores His people Israel, He will plant within their hearts a respect for Him which will know no disobedience but constant surrender and devotion to Him alone.

Some may feel that we are interpreting this passage from Jeremiah too literally. Such is not the case however. Paul would be the first to admit that his brethren after the flesh were not worthy of this future blessing. He maintains that the future blessing for Israel is the result of God's sovereign grace alone. "As concerning the gospel, they are enemies for your sakes; but as touching the election, they are beloved for the fathers' sakes. For the gifts and calling of God are without repentance" (Rom. 11:28, 29).

Basis of Israel's Deliverance

The fact that Israel exists at all is the result of God's sovereign grace. Were they not called in Abraham? "Now the Lord had said unto Abram, Get thee out of thy country, and from thy kindred, and from thy father's house, unto a land that I will shew thee: And I will make of thee a great nation, and I will bless thee and make thy name great; and thou shalt be a blessing. And I will bless them that bless thee, and curse him that curseth thee, and in thee shall all families of the earth be blessed" (Gen. 12:1–3). Furthermore, through Moses, God had told Israel that of themselves they were absolutely nothing. "For thou art an holy people unto the Lord thy God: the Lord hath chosen thee to be a special people unto himself, above all people that are upon the face of the earth. The Lord did not set his love upon you, nor choose you, because ye were more in number than any people; for ye were the fewest of all people; but because the Lord loved you, and because he would keep the oath which he had sworn unto your fathers, hath the Lord brought you out with a mighty hand, and redeemed you out of the house of bondmen, from the hand of Pharaoh, king of Egypt" (Deut. 7:6–8). God distinctly says that Israel was absolutely nothing; they were not a people. He tells us that by His great love He redeemed them in order that they might be a holy and peculiar people unto Him. As we read the Old Testament, we discover why God chose this people for Himself. Through them was to come the Messiah. Through them also were to come the holy Scriptures. And from them was to come the witness to the one and only true God. "Hear, O Israel: The Lord our God is one Lord. And thou shalt love the Lord thy God with all thine heart, and with all thy soul, and with all thy might" (Deut. 6:4, 5).

Did Israel not disobey God? Did they not break His covenant? Do they not deserve to be forgotten? The answer to these three questions is an emphatic yes!

But God does not deal with Israel according to their deserts. He deals with them because of His love for the fathers Abraham, Isaac and Jacob. "But as touching the election, they are beloved for the fathers' sakes."

There can be no doubt of the fact that Israel's rebellion and disobedience grieve the heart of God. Even so, He did not regret that He chose this rebellious and disobedient people to be His own. Again, what is true of us believers on an individual scale will be true of Israel on a national scale. Both we and they can only plead the grace of God. Paul confirms this when he writes, "for the gifts and calling of God are without regret." Looking at his people, Paul was forced to admit that they deserved to be lost. Relying upon God's Word, he knew that they would be delivered. Knowing the law, he could never forget the words which God spoke to Moses, "God is not a man, that he should lie; neither the son of man, that he should repent. Hath he said, and shall he not do it? or hath he spoken, and shall he not make it good?" (Num. 23:19).

XVIII

The Mercy of God

For as ye in times past have not believed God, yet have now obtained mercy through their unbelief: Even so have these also now not believed, that through your mercy they also may obtain mercy. For God hath concluded them all in unbelief, that he might have mercy upon all. (Rom. 11:30–32)

It has been said that the mouth is the billboard of the heart. Certain words indicate the temperament of the person who utters them. Of the many words that Paul uses to preach the gospel, three are outstanding. They are the words "love," "mercy," and "grace." These three words sum up Paul's devotion to the Lord Jesus Christ.

In the text which is before us, Paul uses the word "mercy" three times. He speaks of the mercy which has been extended to us (v. 30). He speaks of the mercy which is extended to the individual Jew (v. 31). He speaks of the mercy which is to be extended to Israel as a nation (v. 32).

What is Mercy?

It is not difficult for us to understand why Paul delights to utter this word "mercy." Throughout all his epistles he informs us that he himself has been the personal object of God's sovereign mercy. He writes to young Timothy, "I thank Christ Jesus our Lord, who hath enabled me, for that he counted me faithful, putting me into the ministry; Who was before a blasphemer, and a persecutor, and injurious: but I obtained mercy, because I did it ignorantly in unbelief" (1 Tim. 1:12, 13).

Our English word "mercy" has to do with compassion, clemency, and forgiveness. It also has reference to the giving of alms, or donations for given causes.

The Mercy of God

It is derived from the Latin *marces* which has to do with pay or a favor. It is a word of the heart, for it is the love of the heart which makes any expression of true mercy possible.

The Greek word *eleos* indicates the need for mercy; it has within it the idea of living from others. We speak of "eleemosynary institutions," such as The Red Cross, The United Fund, The Cancer Society, the Boy Scouts, the church, or any other organization which lives from the offerings of the public.

My research assistant told me the following incident which illustrates clearly our Greek word for mercy. When he was pastor of a church in metropolitan New York, he had a Scotch lady come in each Wednesday to take care of the manse for him. She always brought the children to lunch since the school was just across the street from the parsonage. Without fail, after the grace she would say, "Eat up, it's on the pastor; we do not have to pay for it today." This expression was but an evidence of a Scotsman's thrift. On one of these occasions my assistant said to the woman: "You know, when you say, 'Eat up, it's on the pastor; we do not have to pay for it today!', you make me think of a verse of Scripture from Ephesians, 'But God, who is rich in mercy, for His great love wherewith He loved us' (2:4). Because of His mercy, we can say, "Eat up, it is on the Lord; we do not have to pay for it today." The reason we do not need to pay for it, today nor any other day, is because on the cross the Lord Jesus Christ paid the price for us.

Mercy for Us

As Paul rightly says in our text, "we, as Gentiles, were at one time disobedient to God. We had no use for him whatsoever. We have obtained mercy by means of Israel's unbelief. The Lord Jesus Christ came into the world and was ignored by it. He came to his own people and they rejected him. To those who did receive him he gave the authority to become the sons of God, even to them who believe in him" (John 1:10–12).

Only when we stop to think of what we were before we were redeemed, can we truly appreciate the wealth of God's mercy to us. We were dead in trespasses and sins. Let us not deceive our selves by thinking we were passively dead; we were intensely active—in active rebellion against God. We followed the world as we ignored His Word. We worshipped the creature as we rejected the Creator. We walked according to the manner and customs of this Godless world. By nature, we were selfish as we satisfied the desires of our flesh and of our mind. We endeavored to disregard the fact that we were the children of God's wrath, even as we were hounded by His grace.

CHAPTER XVIII

Against the wealth of our sinful poverty, God placed the wealth of His mercy. Why did He do it? Paul states the answer simply, "Because of his great love for us." Who can measure the greatness of this love? We know it is an impartial love, because John writes, "For God so loved the world that he gave his only begotten Son, that whosoever believeth in him should not perish, but have everlasting life" (John 3:16). Who can measure the height, the depth, the breadth and the length of that little word "so." In His great high priestly prayer, the Lord Jesus Christ measures the greatness of this little word for us. "Neither pray I for these alone, but for them also which shall believe on me through their word,.... and that the world may know that thou hast sent me, *and hast loved them, as thou hast loved me*" (John 17:20–23). Only when we stand in His presence and see Him face to face, shall we really know how God the Father loved God the Son.

Now that we have seen the greatness of God's love as He expressed it in the wealth of His mercy, we must pause for a moment to look at the wealth of grace which motivated it. "In whom we have redemption through his blood, the forgiveness of sins, according to the riches of his grace" (Eph. 1:7). God never saved us according to our poverty; He saved us according to His wealth. God never bartered for our souls on margin; He bought us outright and made us His. To be sure, we needed a Savior who would deliver us from the wages of sin. It took the death of the Lord Jesus Christ to justify us in the presence of God, but the full provision for our salvation was made on the basis of "the riches of his grace."

Someone has well described grace as "help for the helpless, mercy for the undeserving, everything for nothing." It is God's unmerited favor extended to us. The truth of this wonderful word we must never take for granted. Though "everything for nothing" appears to be true, we must never forget that it cost the Lord Jesus Christ everything. It is the death of the Lord Jesus Christ that guarantees God's daily provision for us. "He that spared not his own Son, but delivered him up for us all, how shall he not with him also freely give us all things?" (Rom. 8:32). The word "freely" repeats the grace note which Paul delights to sound. It is a word which might well be translated "absolutely without a cause." God has saved us so that He might be good to us. He has told us that the purpose of our salvation is that He might be kind to us, not only in this age, but in all the ages coming upon us. (Eph. 2:7)

Mercy for Israel

Is such mercy for us alone? Paul answers emphatically, "No!" The same God who has been merciful to the Gentiles, will be merciful to the Jews. The mercy which

The Mercy of God

God has extended to us is but an evidence of the mercy which He will manifest in Israel's restoration. "Even so, have these also now not believed, that through your mercy they also may obtain mercy" (Rom. 11:31)? We must be careful not to misinterpret this verse in terms of personal salvation for individual Jews. We must keep in mind that God is dealing with Jews and Gentiles as ethnic groups here, not as individual men. The verse before us speaks of Israel's national restoration. This is confirmed by Paul's previous testimony. "For if the casting away of them be the reconciling of the world, what shall the receiving of them be, but life from the dead?" (Rom. 11:15). God in sovereign electing grace will restore a nation in a day, even as in this age of grace He brings life out of death to each individual believer. He will do this out of sheer grace because of the greatness of His love in the extension of His mercy. What God is doing for us individually, He will do for Israel nationally.

Israel can never merit this mercy, for she is in rebellious unbelief. In the Greek, the word "unbelief" is a very strong word; it really translates into "disobedience." This disobedience does not spring from mere indifference. The verb form of the word indicates a rebellion, a refusal to be persuaded or to be convinced. It adds up to the spirit of outright stubbornness and open resistance. This kind of disobedience is not born of ignorance; it is born of insolence. Isaiah sets forth the spirit of this rebellion. "Who hath believed our report? And to whom is the arm of the Lord revealed? For he shall grow up before him as a tender plant, and as a root out of a dry ground. He hath no form nor comeliness; and when we shall see him, there is no beauty that we should desire him. He is despised and rejected of men, a man of sorrows, and acquainted with grief; and we hid as it were our faces from him; he was despised and we esteemed him not" (Isa. 53:1–3).

It is in this fifty-third chapter of Isaiah that Messiah's great work as the Paschal Lamb is set forth. "Surely he hath borne our griefs, and carried our sorrows. Yet we did esteem him stricken, smitten of God, and afflicted. But he was wounded for our transgressions, he was bruised for our iniquities; the chastisement of our peace was upon him, and with his stripes we are healed" (Isa. 53:4, 5). In the beginning of the gospel, at the announcement of the birth of the Lord Jesus Christ, God tells us that Jesus came to be Israel's Savior Messiah: "And she shall bring forth a son, and thou shalt call his name Jesus. For he shall save *his people* from their sins" (Matt. 1:21). Paul confirms this by presenting Christ as the new passover: "For even Christ our passover is sacrificed for us" (1 Cor. 5:7).

Isaiah points out that Israel's disobedience was not a matter of ignorance but of insolence. "All we like sheep have gone astray; *we have turned every one to his own way*; and the Lord hath laid on him the iniquity of us all" (Isa. 53:6). This

CHAPTER XVIII

verse should call forth God's wrath; instead, it calls forth His mercy. The iniquities of Israel as well the iniquities of the Gentiles, have been laid on Jesus Christ.

Mercy for All

Someone may raise the question: If God is going to convert Israel as a nation, why should we be interested in witnessing to them now? The answer is quite simple. God is not dealing with nations now; He is dealing with individual men and women. The Lord Jesus Christ came to seek and to save that which was lost. God is dealing with neither Gentiles nor Jews. He is not dealing with the color of a person's skin, nor their academic or financial status. In this present hour, God is only interested in the souls of men. Through the gospel He tells them they are lost in sin, but that they can be saved through the sacrifice of the Lord Jesus Christ on Calvary's cross. Today, we witness to the Jews primarily, as men and women who need to know the Savior. Paul sounds this note. "For I am not ashamed of the gospel of Christ; for it is the power of God unto salvation, to everyone that believeth; to the Jew first, and also to the Greek" (Rom. 1:16). While we rejoice in the glorious hope of Israel's ultimate restoration as a nation, we must not shirk our responsibility to present the gospel of salvation to them now. The Gentile believer who has carefully studied this portion of Paul's epistle to the Romans will not find witnessing to the Jews a dreary obligation, but a privilege. The unbelief which we experience in witnessing to individual Jews will be but a testimony to the mercy of God toward us, and will call forth our gratitude toward Him.

Paul now comes to the final summation of his argument that both Jews and Gentiles have to be objects of God's mercy and love. "For God hath concluded them all in unbelief, that he might have mercy upon all." Our English word "concluded" is a translation of a very picturesque Greek word. Paul actually says that God has "hemmed us in," "imprisoned us," or "shut us up in the place of disobedience." One should think that this would merit His wrath and His total abandonment of us. Paul points out, however, that God concludes us all under sin in order that He might show mercy to us. From our study of this portion of the epistle, we can well understand why we should be on our way to hell, whether we be Jews or Gentiles. What we shall never understand is why we should be on our way to heaven. Who can explain the reason for His love? Who can hope to fathom the depths of His mercy? Who is really worthy of His grace?

No one is worthy, declares the Apostle Paul. Gentiles are no better than Jews, and Jews are no better than Gentiles. "What then? Are we better than they? No, in no wise, For we have before proved both Jews and Gentiles, that they are all under sin; as it is written, There is none righteous, no, not one, there is none that understandeth, there is none that seeketh after God. They are all gone out of the way, they are together become unprofitable; there is none that doeth good, no, not one" (Rom. 3:9–12). Since the Scripture concludes us all under sin, the promise by faith in Jesus Christ is extended to all men that they might believe.

One who understands this passage and has really experienced the redeeming love of God the Father through Jesus Christ the Lord will never be guilty of slandering God with the accusation that He delights in sending people to Hell. There is not a line in the Bible to substantiate this blasphemous canard. Let us not forget that in the garden it was God who sought Adam after the fall. Adam never sought God; he fled from Him. In writing to young Timothy, Paul explains the heart of God. "For this is good and acceptable in the sight of God our Savior; who will have all men to be saved and to come unto the knowledge of the truth. For there is one God and one mediator between God and men, the man Christ Jesus; who gave himself a ransom for all, to be testified in due time" (1 Tim. 2:3–6).

God is the God of mercy. He expressed this mercy in times past when He cared for His ancient people Israel, bringing them from the bondage of Egypt into the land of promise. God is the God of mercy in this present time, having provided the gospel of the Lord Jesus Christ by which we may come to the knowledge of the truth as it is in Him. God will be the God of mercy in the future as He restores His ancient people, who are now in disobedient unbelief, to a position of glory and fellowship with Him.

XIX

The Mind of God

O the depth of the riches both of the wisdom and knowledge of God! How unsearchable are his judgments, and his ways past finding out! For who hath known the mind of the Lord? or who hath been his counsellor? Or who hath first given to him, and it shall be recompensed unto him again? For of him, and through him, and to him, are all things: to whom be glory forever. Amen. (Rom. 11:33–36).

In this last section of Romans, chapters nine through eleven, Paul breaks forth in a paean of praise to God for His wonderful works to the children of men. God's mercy, love and grace, when clearly understood, always call forth a song of joy. When we began our study of this part of the epistle, Paul was in sorrow for his brethren after the flesh; now he is in joy because of the hope that is theirs in Christ Jesus.

In his song of praise, the apostle sings of the mind of God. What mind but God's mind could think out a plan of salvation that would redeem ruined man? Who, but God could display wisdom that would make full provision for the needs of all mankind? Who else, but God, would care for those who hated Him?

Many men have been baffled by the mind of God. Through the ages, philosophers have tried to understand it. Each in turn has failed in his attempt. For them God is but an unknown "X", at best a great "Idea," at worst a mythical concept of our own creation. Men have ignored the way to God and, as a consequence, they have never found Him.

Paul's God of whom he sings is not the God of philosophy or theology. His God is the God and Father of our Lord Jesus Christ who satisfies the longing heart. Of Him David sang, "Oh that men would praise the Lord for his goodness and for his wonderful works to the children of men! For he satisfieth the longing soul and filleth the hungry soul with goodness" (Ps. 107:8, 9). Philosophers may argue over their ignorance about God; Paul chooses to revel in His goodness.

In the passage before us, Paul tells of why the mind of God is a mystery to man and how man may know it.

The Mind of God

First of all, Paul points out that the mind of God is infinite. With this the philosophers agree. They have reached their conclusion through ignorance; the apostle arrives at his conclusion through Divine revelation and personal experience. He declares, "O the depth of the wealth, both of the wisdom and of the experience of God! How undiscoverable are His judgments, and how untraceable are His roads" (Rom. 11:33, Greek). Here, Paul speaks of the wealth of God's wisdom and knowledge. This is to the point since in the previous passages he has just been discussing God's providence as shown in the history of the Gentiles and the nation of Israel. For Paul, God was not an absent Creator, indifferent to His world and its people. His knowledge, of which Paul speaks, is not a mere academic knowledge such as is common to a worldly intelligentsia. As the Greek word indicates, this knowledge is born of personal experience and personal participation. What more can express this personal knowledge of God than the words "love," "mercy," and "grace?" The very word "wisdom" confirms God's interest in His creation. "Wisdom" is a practical word which applies the knowledge it knows. Furthermore it furnishes the reason for any given action. His is a wisdom born of His good pleasure.

Paul's God was never poor. We have seen how He was rich in mercy and rich in love. Here Paul tells us that His God is also rich in wisdom and knowledge. These are not idle concepts for the apostle; they are an expression of an experience of saving grace. He condemns the world for rejecting the wealth of God's goodness. "And thinkest thou this, O man, that judgest them which do such things and doest the same, that thou shalt escape the judgment of God? Or despisest thou the riches of his goodness and forbearance and longsuffering; not knowing that the goodness of God leadeth thee to repentance? But after thy hardness and impenitent heart treasurest up unto thyself wrath against the day of wrath and revelation of the righteous judgment of God" (Rom. 2:3–5). He revels in God's sovereignty and the riches of His glory (Rom. 9:23). Only a man redeemed by God can avoid the pitfalls of philosophical blindness as he rests in the unsearchable riches of God in Christ. Paul claimed to be one of these men (Eph. 3:8).

This is not a selfish claim, however. All men may claim this privilege if they come to Christ for salvation. Furthermore, the unknown principalities and powers are watching the drama of God's great wisdom on display as His sovereign grace works out salvation. God has ordained the church to be the theatre of His universe. "And to enlighten all men as to the dispensation of the mystery, which from the begining of the ages has been hid in God, the one who created all things; in order that now might be made known to the principalities and authorities in the heavens, *through the church*, the many-sided wisdom of God; according to the purpose of the ages which he projected in Jesus Christ our Lord" (Eph. 3:9–11, Greek). Though Paul chooses to emphasize one side of God, wisdom and knowledge; this passage shows that he was not ignorant of the fact that God's wisdom and knowledge is "many-sided." He merely chose the side about which he knew most—the wisdom of God in salvation. This passage shows that God's wisdom and knowledge has its cosmic side as well.

No wonder Paul, the theologian-philosopher, sings. He insists in looking at God's wisdom through the eyes of a sinner redeemed. For he has a part in this great cosmic drama of grace. He is a participant in this display of God's wisdom. The unknown cosmic intelligences are merely observers of it.

God's Uniqueness

Not only is God infinite, He is unique as well. "For who hath known the mind of the Lord? or who hath been his counsellor? or who hath first given to him, and it shall be recompensed to him again?" (Rom. 11:34, 35). Paul did not need to search far for an answer. He remembered Isaiah: "For my thoughts are not your thoughts, neither are your ways my ways, saith the Lord. For as the heavens are higher than the earth, so are my ways higher than your ways, and my thoughts than your thoughts" (Isa. 55:8, 9). No man has ever known God's mind! Who was there to be His teacher? Who was there to advise Him? "Who hath directed the Spirit of the Lord or, being his counsellor, hath taught Him? With whom took he counsel, and who instructed him and taught him in the path of judgment, and taught him knowledge, and showed to him the way of understanding? Behold, the nations are as a drop of a bucket, and are counted as the small dust of the balance; behold, he taketh up the isles as a very little thing." (Isa. 40:13–15). If the nations are less than a water-drop, and man is but balance-dust in God's sight, what wisdom can they contribute to Him?

Oh, if we could only learn that God does not need us but that we need him. This was the message of Paul to the intellects of his day. Paul did not try to make unnecessary concessions to them when he witnessed to them. He did not whittle God down to the size of their peanut-size minds; he demanded that they change—be converted—in order that they might grow up into the mind of God. Hear him speak to the Athenians on Mars' Hill. "God that made the world and all things therein, seeing that he is Lord of heaven and earth, dwelleth not in temples made with hands; Neither is worshipped with men's hands, *as though he needed anything*, seeing he giveth to all life and breath and all things. For in him we live, and move, and have our being; as certain also of your own poets have said, For we are also his offspring" (Acts 17:24, 25, 28).

Matters may not be as hopeless as they appear. God has planted eternity in men's hearts (Eccles. 3:11 marg.). The wise Greeks of Athens confirmed this truth. Though they had their Pantheon, they were not taking any chances in overlooking a god they did not know. Paul chides them, "Ye men of Athens, I perceive that in all things ye are too superstitious. For as I passed by, and beheld your devotions, I found an altar with this inscription 'To The Unknown God.' Whom, therefore, ye ignorantly worship, him declare I unto you" (Acts 17:22, 23). Philosophy is not sufficient to deal with the ultimate issues of life. Men are forced to recognize God, even against their will. All the philosophers of the past and present bear testimony to being haunted by the "unknown" God. My assistant tells this story about his class in the philosophy of religion, in one of the graduate schools of an eastern university. They were discussing a certain book where the author had thrown God out of his considerations in the first chapter. However, in the last chapter of the book, the writer seemed to sneak God back into his pages. My assistant asked the reason for this treatment of God. "Why was He brought in now, since the author of the text had no use for God in the greater part of the book?" The professor was quite frank in his reply (since he knew the author of the book under discussion, his answer had some significance), "The author doubtless expected to die and he was just playing it safe." With Paul we would insist that a sign of a good philosophy is this: Can you die with it as well as live by it? Man's heart may be in rebellion, but as long as God troubles temporal man with eternity we can feel encouraged in our witness for Him.

God is Ever-Present

Another reason the apostle Paul stresses the personal side of God's wisdom and knowledge is simply that God is always with us. He is not an absentee Creator Who started the universe and has now left it to run its course. He created it; He governs and sustains it; He has given all things a purpose which is to glorify Him. Paul declares this to be true. "For of him, through him, and to him, are all things; to whom be glory forever. Amen" (Rom. 11:36). In this brief passage, Paul smashes a number of philosophical idols. Matter is not eternal, because it is created; thus materialism is questioned. God created all things; thus mechanical evolution is put to rest. He sustains all things; thus purposeless evolution is set aside along with any other system that would deny that the world is held together by the active intervention of a transcendent, immanent God. All things are for Him; thus to hold the idea of a purposeless universe is shattered. Space does not permit us to take each of these phrases and trace them through the Word of God. If one should take the time to do it, he would discover that the fact and the proof for each phrase exists in the Scripture.

Why a Mystery?

Why is the nature of God's mind such a mystery? Why have the best minds of men not been able to discover the nature of God and His wisdom? The answer is so simple that men reject it. Sin is the answer. When I say sin, I want us to consider it in its truly Greek sense. The Greek word for "sin" is *hamartia*. It is taken from the world of sports, having to do with archery. It envisions an archer in place, who deflects his aim and misses the mark. He sins by missing the mark. His purpose was to hit the bull's eye. The world is made up of bad archers. "For all have sinned, and come short of the glory of God" (Rom. 3:23).

We were created in the likeness and image of God. We were created in knowledge, righteousness and true holiness (Col. 3:10, cf. Eph. 4:23, 24). As rational creatures we could communicate with God. As moral creatures we could live like God. As holy creatures we could please God. All this was gained for us in Adam. Furthermore, in Adam, God planned that man should reign for Him on earth (Gen. 1:26–28), but Adam decided to be God himself. Though Eve was deceived by Satan, God held Adam responsible. Through this rebellion, man, through Adam, lost the high privilege of ruling with God and the opportunity of really knowing God.

Man still could know God if it were not for his vanity. God has endowed all men with the light of common grace. Men reject it, preferring the darkness of their evil deeds rather than to have them exposed to light (John 3:19–21). In his rebellion against God, man has substituted the creature for the Creator; he has substituted the worship of man for the worship of God. He has chosen death instead of life. He has degenerated to the worship and the life of a beast. (Rom. 1:21–23).

The Mind of God

Knowing His Mind

How is it possible for degenerate man to know the mind of God? How is it possible for a dog to know a man? There are many dogs who think quite highly of their masters. They show high intelligence in their relationships; they display great devotion; and they are indeed faithful to those they love. But at best, whether it be the devotion of a thoroughbred or the faithfulness of a mutt, it is still the expression of a dog. For a dog to know a man, he must possess a human nature. A canine nature simply will not do. Man, as a degenerate sinner, may know God in the same way a dog knows man. There is only one way to know God and that is through a Godlike nature. This is offered to us in the Gospel. "But as many as received him, to them gave he the authority to become *the sons of God*, even to them who believe on his name; who are born, not of blood, nor of the will of the flesh, nor of man, but of God." (John. 1:12, 13). The difference between man and God is not one of degree, it is of kind. No one would ever class a dog as a form of man. To know the mind of God we must first partake of the nature of God.

The second provision God made for us to know Him was to send the Lord Jesus Christ to earth to make Him known. As the *logos* of God, he embodies God's thought and the treasury of His wisdom and knowledge for us. (Col. 2:3, 9). He is the alphabet of God who unfolds God to us. No one will ever see God apart from Jesus Christ. "No man hath seen God at any time; the only begotten son, who is in the bosom of the Father, he hath declared [spelled out] him." (John 1:18). This is why the Lord Jesus declares: "I am the way, the truth, and the life; no man cometh unto the Father, but by me" (John 14:6).

Finding God

We have seen that God has made a two-fold provision for man to know His mind: the provision to become a partaker of the Divine nature, and the coming of God into the world in the person of Jesus Christ. There is now an invitation extended to man from God, to believe His word, not through blind faith, but through living experience. "If any man will do his will, he shall know of the doctrine, whether it be of God, or whether I speak of myself" (John 7:17). All God asks is for a person to expose himself to His word without bias or prejudice. Our Lord sets up the experiment. Submit yourself to the Word, and the Word will prove itself to you. It will prove to be the Word of God, not the Word of man. You must follow its rules; you cannot violate them.

CHAPTER XIX

It is very important to follow carefully the laws of a chemical experiment. You cannot decide to make the experiment according to your whims. You must make it according to the laws of the chemicals involved. Brilliant though you be, one little slip may cost you a hand or even your head. To avoid spiritual explosions, one must follow the directions of the great Chemist, the Lord Jesus Christ.

When one becomes a partaker of the Divine nature, when one heeds the invitation and studies God's alphabet, the Lord Jesus Christ, then one is ready to glorify God. This is man's true end. This is the way to the wisdom and knowledge of God. In this knowledge, one can sing his praises as did the great apostle.

ω ἡ δοξα
εἰς τοὺς αἰῶνας τῶν αἰώνων
ἀμην

www.ingramcontent.com/pod-product-compliance
Lightning Source LLC
Chambersburg PA
CBHW020357170426
43200CB00005B/201